GROWING MONEY

A COMPLETE
INVESTING GUIDE FOR KIDS

written by
Gail Karlitz

created by
Debbie Honig

PSS!
PRICE STERN SLOAN
An Imprint of Penguin Group (USA) Inc.

To Jennifer Kate Buhler, who will always be my very best investment.—G.K.

To my parents, Louis and Mary, who taught me to vary my investments, and my husband, Steven, who had the idea to purchase stocks for kid special occasions and frame the certificates as artwork, a double investment!—D.H.

Acknowledgments

Special thanks to everyone at NYSE Euronext, especially Ray Pellecchia and Michael Rutigliano, William Chang (Roaring Brook Management), and Pedro Ramirez (Belray Asst Management). Your time, patience, and wealth of knowledge were invaluable in creating this book.—Gail Karlitz

PRICE STERN SLOAN
Published by the Penguin Group
Penguin Group (USA) Inc., 375 Hudson Street, New York, New York 10014, USA
Penguin Group (Canada), 90 Eglinton Avenue East, Suite 700,
Toronto, Ontario M4P 2Y3, Canada (a division of Pearson Penguin Canada Inc.)
Penguin Books Ltd., 80 Strand, London WC2R 0RL, England
Penguin Group Ireland, 25 St. Stephen's Green, Dublin 2, Ireland (a division of Penguin Books Ltd.)
Penguin Group (Australia), 250 Camberwell Road, Camberwell, Victoria 3124, Australia
(a division of Pearson Australia Group Pty. Ltd.)
Penguin Books India Pvt. Ltd., 11 Community Centre, Panchsheel Park, New Delhi—110 017, India
Penguin Group (NZ), 67 Apollo Drive, Rosedale, North Shore 0632, New Zealand (a division of Pearson New Zealand Ltd.)
Penguin Books (South Africa) (Pty.) Ltd., 24 Sturdee Avenue, Rosebank, Johannesburg 2196, South Africa

Penguin Books Ltd., Registered Offices: 80 Strand, London WC2R 0RL, England

Library of Congress Control Number: 2010013441

ISBN 978-0-8431-9905-5

10 9 8 7 6 5 4 3 2 1

CONTENTS

BEFORE
YOU START

There are many different ways to make money grow. That's what this book is all about. You'll learn about savings accounts, bonds, stocks, and mutual funds, and how to pick the investments that are right for you.

Here are just a few things to keep in mind when you read this book.

- Because you are a kid, the law refers to you as a "minor." That means that if you want to buy stocks or bonds, your parent or your guardian must be involved. You cannot buy stocks or bonds yourself until you are eighteen.

- This book tells you about the kinds of things that you should think about when you make money decisions. But do not let any book tell you exactly what to do with your money. You and your parents should always use your own judgment.

🍀 By the time you read this book, many things may have changed. Every year, some companies change their names or the symbols for their stocks. Companies buy other companies, or they sell off parts of themselves. New companies are formed, and some old companies go out of business.

🍀 Many examples in this book use the names of real companies. That doesn't mean we are recommending that you should invest in them—or that you should not invest in them. We've just used them as examples because they are companies that are probably familiar to you.

We hope you have fun with this book. Most of all, we hope that when you are ready, you will be able to invest wisely, as well as successfully.

CHAPTER ONE

WHERE DO YOU KEEP YOUR MONEY?

Let's agree on one thing right from the start: If you want to make your money grow, the worst place to keep it is in the pocket of your jeans. You know what happens: You either spend it right away or forget to take it out of your pocket. Eventually, your jeans end up on the floor, right there with the rest of the clothes you've worn all week, your schoolbooks, the blanket you kicked off your bed, and other assorted treasures.

What always happens the day your room is the messiest? That's right! Your mom makes you clean it, and fast! And what happens to the jeans with the money? You've got it. They end up in the laundry. And then the money is lost and gone forever.

But what about keeping your money in your room—in a safe place, like a piggy bank?

There are a lot of good reasons to keep your money safe in your room.

WHY DO BANKS LOOK LIKE PIGS?

Why *do* people put money in banks shaped like pigs? Are pigs known for being careful with their money?

The truth is that a long time ago, people had inexpensive pots or jugs in their kitchens that were made of a common clay known as pygg. When people had some extra money, they would put it into these containers. Eventually, the containers became known as pygg banks, or pyggy banks. Later, someone had a great idea and began to make banks in the shape of pigs!

For one thing, it's right there when you need it. You can get to it quickly and easily. Another good thing is that you always know exactly how much money you have. You can take it out at any time and count it.

Of course, the very reason keeping your money in your room is good can *also* be the reason keeping your money in your room is bad. Let's suppose you are saving your money for something big, like a new bike. Your savings are growing nicely. You're up to $35, and then . . . you see a great baseball cap that you really want to buy. It's only $15. And it's so cool!

What a dilemma! You know that you shouldn't touch your bike money. But there it is, in your room, in that piggy bank. It's calling to you: "Come and get me. You know you want to spend me. I'm right here waiting for you. Come get me now, and you'll have that cap today!" Boy, that money sure knows how to be mighty tempting! Money in a piggy bank is money that is easy to spend.

Another thing about keeping your money in a piggy bank is that the amount of money you have is never more than what you have put into the piggy bank. If you put in $5 every month, after a year you will have $60. After ten years, you will have $600. No more, no less.

Now, it's always a good idea to save money. So what's bad about saving money this way? Well, over time, the price of everything—from a pack of gum to a new bike—goes up. This is called **inflation**. It means that in ten years, $600 won't buy nearly as much stuff as it will now.

Think about what has happened to the buying power of money. In 1960, a kid with a quarter could buy a slice of pizza for 15¢ and a soda for 10¢. Today, you'd probably need at least $4 to buy the same meal! In 1960, a kid who had saved $6 could buy movie tickets for himself and four friends, and then buy each person a popcorn and a drink. Today, that same $6 would not buy a movie ticket for even one person! A really generous kid could use his $6 to buy one tub of popcorn for everyone to share.

Many adults love to talk about the good old days and how low prices were back then. They sometimes forget that incomes were pretty low then, too. In 1960, the **average** income per person in this country was $2,283 per year! By 2008, the average income per person was $34,946.

THEN AND NOW

Ask your parents or grandparents about the costs of some things when they were young. Then look up the costs of those things today.

Some things may cost more now; other things may cost less. Here are some ideas.

	THEN	NOW
New car	_____	_____
Sunday newspaper	_____	_____
Jeans	_____	_____
Sneakers	_____	_____
Candy bar	_____	_____
Ice-cream cone	_____	_____
Movie ticket	_____	_____
Calculator	_____	_____
TV	_____	_____
Computer	_____	_____

SOMETHING TO THINK ABOUT

Burger King opened its first restaurant in 1954. A burger was 18¢, and a milkshake was 18¢. What does that meal cost today?

In addition to the fact that a specific amount of money loses some of its buying power as time goes by, another reason people usually don't keep their money at home is space. If you have a lot of money (which would be a really nice problem to have!), it gets a little hard to find places for it all. A million dollars in dollar bills:

🐛 laid end to end would run for 97 miles.

🐛 stacked on top of one another would be 358 feet high—as high as a thirty-five-story skyscraper.

🐛 would weigh more than a ton—2,202 pounds, to be exact.

Of course, no one would really keep a million dollar bills around. They would at least trade them in for ten thousand hundred-dollar bills!

Paper money is printed by the United States Bureau of Engraving and Printing in Washington, D.C., and in Fort Worth, Texas. In 2009, the bureau printed an average of twenty-six million bills per day. Our government used to print money in larger amounts than hundred-dollar bills, but it no longer does. They printed $500, $1,000, $5,000, and even $10,000 bills, mainly for transfers between banks, but electronic transfers have made these bills obsolete. Some of those large bills are still around—it was estimated in May 2009 that about 165,732 $1,000, 342 $5,000 bills, and 336 $10,000 bills were still in circulation! You probably won't see them, though. They are considered valuable antiques, and most of them are in private collections or in safe-deposit boxes. People who want to sell their $10,000 bills can get up to $140,000 for each one!

HOW LONG DOES MONEY LAST?

The Bureau of Engraving and Printing produces additional paper money to replace money that is damaged, destroyed, lost, or just plain worn out. Denominations that are used more frequently have shorter life spans than those that are not used very often.

DENOMINATION	AVERAGE LIFE SPAN
$1 bill	21 months
$5 bill	16 months
$10 bill	18 months
$20 bill	24 months
$50 bill	55 months
$100 bill	89 months
Coins	About 30 years

TRIVIA

It costs 6.4 cents to print each bill! In 2009, 7.7 billion bills were printed. Here's how much coins cost:
Penny—1.26 cents
Nickel—7.7 cents
Dime—4 cents
Quarter—10 cents
Dollar (coins)—16 cents

WHO'S WHO ON OUR MONEY

$1.00 ....George Washington (first US president)

$2.00 ....Thomas Jefferson (third US president)

$5.00 ....Abraham Lincoln (sixteenth US president)

$10.00...Alexander Hamilton (first US treasury secretary)

$20.00 ....Andrew Jackson (seventh US president)

$50.00 ....Ulysses S. Grant (eighteenth US president)

$100.00 ....Benjamin Franklin (one of the Founding Fathers)

$500.00 (not printed since 1946) ....William McKinley (twenty-fifth US president)

$1,000.00 (not printed since 1946).........Grover Cleveland (twenty-second and twenty-fourth US president)

$5,000.00 (not printed since 1946)........James Madison (fourth US president)

$10,000.00 (not printed since 1946) ....Salmon P. Chase (twenty-fifth US treasury secretary)

$100,000.00 (only from 12/34–1/35)....Woodrow Wilson (twenty-eighth US president)

SPECIAL DOLLAR COINS

Beginning in 2009, the reverse side of the Sacagawea coin, a dollar coin, will have a different image honoring Native Americans each year.

Beginning in 2010, new dollar coins are being issued with the picture of an American president on the front (or *obverse*) and the Statue of Liberty on the reverse. Four different coins will be issued each year, honoring the presidents in the order in which they served.

YOU CAN MAKE MONEY WITH YOUR MONEY

It just doesn't make sense to keep your money at home. You're tempted to spend it, and the prices of the things you want keep going up. The longer you hold on to your money, the less it's worth. And, if you did save a fortune, you'd break your back trying to lift it all!

Wait! Don't rush out to spend all your money right now! There are many ways you can save your money so that the amount you put in actually grows, even if you don't add a cent more. When you do that, you are making your money earn more money for you. You are an **investor**.

GET YOUR OWN MONEY RIGHT FROM THE SOURCE!

Did you know that you can buy uncut sheets of dollar bills straight from the printing presses at the Bureau of Engraving and Printing? You can buy some old shredded money there, too.

WELCOME TO THE WIDE WORLD OF INVESTING

All investors hope to get paid for letting other people use their money for a while. Banks, companies, cities, and even countries all need to go to investors—lots of investors—to get the money they need.

THE MOST COMMON INVESTMENT CHOICES

There are many ways to invest money. The most common ways are in savings accounts at banks, in **bonds**, in **stocks**, and in **mutual funds**.

Banks pay you for keeping your money in a savings account. The bank uses your money while it's in the account. If you want to take out some or all of your money, you may do that at any time. You can also deposit more money into your account at any time.

After you open a savings account at a bank, you'll want to keep track of how much money you have in your account. Your bank provides that information to you in different ways. If you want, you can wait for them to send you a statement every month or every quarter (every three months). Or you may choose to look at your account information online at the bank's website. That is the fastest way to know exactly what is happening in your account.

The statement for each of your accounts includes a record of every deposit and every withdrawal you made. You may also see extra money that the bank has deposited into your account. That extra money is called **interest**. The bank is paying you that extra money because you are letting them use the money in your account.

Bonds are loans to companies or governments. The company or government that borrows your money promises to pay you back by a specific date and also to pay you interest for the use of your money.

When you invest in bonds, you may get a bond certificate. The bond certificate spells out the details of the bond: how much money has been borrowed, how much interest you will be paid for the use of your money, and the deadline for paying you back.

Many people give US savings bonds as gifts to newborn babies or as birthday presents to kids. By buying these savings bonds, people are lending money to our country to help it continue to grow.

Stocks are small pieces (or shares) of companies. People who own stock in a company are called **shareholders**. When you are a shareholder, the company may share some of its profits with you . . . if the company has profits.

When you buy stock in a company, you are not lending money to the company. Companies do not promise to pay back the money they get from selling shares of their stock. If you do want your money back, you may try to sell your stock to someone else. When you sell your stock, the price of the stock may be much higher than it was when you bought it. If that happens, you will make a lot of money on the sale. But the price of the stock may also be lower than it was when you bought it. If that happens, you will lose money if you sell it.

Mutual funds are collections of lots of different stocks or bonds. A fund manager chooses a group of stocks (or bonds) for the collection. When you buy shares in a mutual fund, you and many other people each own a portion of this whole collection, but no one in the group owns any specific stock or bond. With mutual funds, as with individual stocks, you can make or lose money.

The four most common investments (bank accounts, bonds, stocks, and mutual funds) are different from one another in several ways.

ARE ALL INVESTMENTS RISKY?

One thing to think about in deciding what kind of investment to make is how much of a **risk** you are willing to take. In the investing world, risk is the chance that you may lose some or all of the money that you invest. Usually investments that have more risk also have a higher chance of making a lot of money for you.

Some investments, like savings accounts or US savings bonds, involve almost no risk. You know exactly how much your money will grow, and you will not lose any of the money you invest. Some investments are very risky. When you put money into a high-risk investment, like buying stock in a brand-new company, your money may grow a lot. Or you may lose it all.

So how do you know how risky an investment is? You'll learn more about that in Chapter Eight.

Another thing to think about in choosing an investment is how long you can leave your money in that investment. Some investments are good for people who can wait a long time for their money to grow. Other investments are good for people who want to be able to take out their money whenever they need it. People who want easy access to their money look for investments with high **liquidity**.

So where should you invest your money? Have you heard the story about the girl who was taking eggs from her family's farm to sell at the market? On her way, the handle on her basket broke. When the basket landed on the ground, all the eggs cracked. The girl made no money, and she learned a lesson: Never put all your eggs in one basket.

Most financial experts agree with that motto. They usually advise each person to have several different kinds of investments. How much of your money you put in each type of investment will be up to you. It all depends on how much risk you want to take and how long you plan to leave your money invested.

Have you ever heard of a baseball or basketball team that won every game in the season? Probably not! It's the same with investing. You can't win them all. No matter how hard you try, you won't pick a winner every time. When you **diversify** (make different kinds of investments) there is a good chance that some of your investments will make money, even if others don't. You will have less risk of losing all of your money.

Investing can be lots of fun. You should invest in the kinds of things that interest you. If seeing your investment go up and down in value very often will make you nervous, you might want to put only a little money into high-risk investments. If you think you will be bored with investments that are predictable, then you should put more of your money in high-risk investments.

WHAT KIND OF INVESTOR ARE YOU?

Right now, you're not old enough to make investments on your own. You need a parent to do your investing for you. But it's never too early to learn about investments or what kind of investor you want to be.

There are all kinds of investors, just as there are all kinds of people. Some people enjoy taking chances. They are like the people who are eager to try bungee jumping. They are risk lovers. Others want to be safe and sure. They are like the people who won't go to a movie until at least five people they know say they liked it. Those people are risk avoiders. Most people are somewhere in the middle.

KNOW YOURSELF

Take this short quiz to find out what kind of investor you are. Don't be nervous—the quiz is fun. There are no right or wrong answers, and you can't pass or fail. It's important to be honest with yourself—don't pretend to be somebody else. (You might want to have your parents or friends take the same quiz. See whether their attitudes about money are the same as yours.)

WHAT KIND OF INVESTOR ARE YOU?

1. You are offered a chance to be part of the first colony on the moon. You:
   a) ask how soon the flight leaves and go home to pack.
   b) agree to be part of the setup team . . . *if* you can come home after six months.
   c) stay on Earth and enjoy breathing without an oxygen tank.

2. Last month, you went to a new restaurant. Since then, you haven't stopped thinking about how great your meal was. You go back this month, and the waiter recommends the special of the day: alligator tail with artichoke sauce. You:
   a) order the same wonderful meal you had last time.
   b) go for the special of the day.
   c) convince your friend to order the special so you can try it.

3. In the music store, you see a new CD. You never have heard of the group, but the sign over the display says they're the hottest band of the century. You:
   a) buy it so you can be the first in your school to discover a new sound.
   b) ask the manager if there's a demo you can listen to.
   c) look for something by a group that you know you like.

4. You're on a TV game show, and you just won $3,000 to decorate your room any way you want. Now you have to decide whether to keep the money or trade it for the secret prize. The secret prize may be a rubber chicken, or it may be a check for a million dollars! You:

a) go for the secret prize—if you don't get the million dollars, you can work on a comedy routine with the rubber chicken.

b) keep the money and plan your new room.

c) do whatever most of the audience votes for you to do.

5. You and your friends are at the brand-new town pool. There is a *very* high diving board that hasn't been tried out yet. You:

a) stick to the low diving board, showing off the cannonball skills you perfected last summer.

b) rush to be the first in line to try out the high board.

c) wait until a few of your friends use it and see what they think.

6. It's the very end of the fourth quarter of the big basketball game. Your team is two points down, and you have the ball. You:

a) pass it to Slam Dunk Sammy, who most likely will score two points to tie the game.

b) pass it to Long Shot Louie, who might score three points to win.

c) pass it to Captain Carl and let him decide who should get it.

7. Your mom won a sales contest at work. The prize is a family trip to Big Kahuna Island in the South Pacific. Big Kahuna is a tropical paradise, but it has a huge volcano right in the middle of it. There's a one-in-five-hundred chance that the volcano will erupt sometime this year. You:

a) agree to go to the island, but make your parents promise you will stay as far from the volcano as possible.

b) plead with your mother to give the trip to someone else.

c) get ready to go and hope that your family will agree to camp out on the most beautiful spot on the island—the top of the huge volcano.

8. Your parents finally agree that you can have a cell phone for your birthday. They offer to buy you a very basic phone, the kind with no games, no text messaging, and no Internet access. You:

a) pass on their offer and hope your grandparents or favorite aunt feel more generous.

b) offer to do some chores to make enough money to contribute to a better phone.

c) thank them and take the phone they have selected. After all, a plain phone is better than no phone.

9. You go to the movie theater with your friend to catch the new horror movie you've both been dying to see for weeks. Unfortunately, you mixed up the show times and you arrive an hour late. You:

a) go to the movie your friend insists she's heard is good, even though it looks weird and boring to you.

b) spot a cool-looking poster for a new movie that neither of you has heard of, but decide to go anyway.

c) buy tickets for the movie you and your friend saw a couple of weeks ago—it wasn't that great, but you could sit through it again.

10. It's almost time for grades to be in, and your teacher asks you to stay after class. At this point, your math grade averages out to a C+. Your teacher gives you the following options. Which will you choose? You:

a) can take a pop quiz on the spot, and, if you do well, you can bring your grade up to a B+, but if you do poorly, your grade could fall to a C-.

b) can agree to take home some extra-credit work that can't hurt your grade but could bring it up to only a B-.

c) can retake one of the tests you bombed, which could bring your grade up to a B or down to a C.

Now, see how many points you get for each answer.

SCORES

1. a=5	b=2	c=1	6. a=1	b=5	c=2
2. a=1	b=5	c=2	7. a=2	b=1	c=5
3. a=5	b=2	c=1	8. a=5	b=2	c=1
4. a=5	b=1	c=2	9. a=2	b=5	c=1
5. a=1	b=5	c=2	10. a=5	b=1	c=2

Your total score:_____

38–50 points: Risk Lover. Taking a chance is exciting. Whether your decision turns out to be right or wrong is not that important to you. The result may be great or awful, but the chance of it being great is worth it. Risk lovers are often referred to as aggressive investors.

20–37 points: Moderate Risk Taker. You enjoy taking a chance, but you try to find out as much as you can first. You are comfortable with a little risk, but not too much. People like you are often known as moderate investors.

10–19 points: Risk Avoider. You like to know what is going to happen. Taking a chance makes you feel nervous and uncomfortable. You want to be as sure as you can that you don't make any huge mistakes. People who are uncomfortable with a lot of risk are known as conservative investors.

You are a (circle one):

☘ RISK LOVER

☘ MODERATE RISK TAKER

☘ RISK AVOIDER

INVESTING FOR YOUR PERSONALITY

Now that you know a little bit about your investing personality, you can start to explore some of the different ways to invest and see which one suits you best. As you learn about each type of investing, you should think about these questions:

- Could I end up with less money than I started with?
- How quickly can I get my money back?
- Does this investment match my investing personality?
- How can I check out what I need to know about this investment?

HOW LIKELY IS IT?

Odds of being a twin: 1 in 90
Odds of being struck by lightning in your lifetime: 1 in 6,250
Odds of being struck by lightning this year: 1 in 500,000
Odds of becoming president: 1 in 10 million
Odds of becoming an astronaut: 1 in 13.2 million
Odds of winning a Powerball Jackpot: 1 in 195 million

There are some investments that have very little risk, where you know that almost certainly you will not lose the money you start with. With low-risk investments, you will earn some more money, and you usually know how much. Lending money to the United States government is a good example of a low-risk investment. You can be sure that our government will be in business for a long time and that it will pay its debts. That investment is very safe, but you will earn only a small amount on it.

How can you invest in the United States? One way is to buy US savings bonds. When you read Chapter Five, you will learn about treasury bonds, notes, and bills, which are other things you can invest in to lend money to our country.

HOW QUICKLY CAN I GET MY MONEY BACK?

When you keep your money in your room, you can get to it very quickly. Some investments are also like that: You can take your money out whenever you want. Most accounts at savings banks are very liquid—you can withdraw as much of your money as you want, whenever you want. There is also a special kind of savings account, called a **certificate of deposit (CD)**, that pays a higher rate of interest if you agree that you will not take your money out of the account for a certain amount of time (anywhere from thirty days to ten years or more).

There are investments (some stocks, for example) whose values go up and down a lot. Those investments are said to be very volatile. **Volatility** can be a problem if the investment is at a very low point just when you need your money. When you know that you won't need your money for a long time, a low point is not as much of a problem. If you are in fifth grade now and you are saving for college, you have the time to wait until your investment goes up again.

CHAPTER FOUR

4

THE LOWDOWN ON SAVINGS BANKS

Savings banks keep your money safe for you. You are very unlikely to lose your money, and spending it all right away is hard, since you have to go to the bank or an automatic teller machine (ATM) to withdraw it.

Savings banks are unlike piggy banks in two important ways. First of all, savings banks pay you for keeping your money there. Secondly, the money that you deposit in a savings account is not really in the bank building where you make your deposit. In fact, banks usually don't keep huge amounts of cash in their buildings. Banks use your deposits to earn more money for themselves.

Banks do keep some money that people have deposited, but most of the money is invested in different ways so the bank can earn more money. Banks lend money to customers who want to buy homes or cars, send their children to college, or even start new businesses.

What if you want to take your money out of the bank? Not to worry. You can always get your money, although for very large amounts you may have to give the bank a few days' notice. That gives them time to get extra cash from another branch or from the money they are keeping in a Federal Reserve Bank vault.

What if everyone wants to take out all their money on the same day? You don't have to worry about that, either. Our government guarantees your deposits are safe. A bank that would not be able to meet all of its obligations can be closed and taken over by the **Federal Deposit Insurance Corporation (FDIC)**. The FDIC will either sell the bank to a stronger one or take over the bank's operations itself for a while. Either way, the depositors are guaranteed to get their deposits back, up to the FDIC limit. In Chapter Eight, we'll learn more about what causes a bank to fail and how that can affect investments.

From 2006 until the end of 2012, the FDIC will insure each depositor for up to $250,000. If you have more than $250,000 (lucky you!), just put it in more than one bank. Your $250,000 will be insured in

QUICK QUIZ

The government tells banks how much of their total deposits they have to have available. That money can be in any of the bank's branches or in the vault at a Federal Reserve Bank. For the largest banks, that amount is about:
a) 10 percent.
b) 50 percent.
c) 90 percent.

Answer: a) 10 percent.

TRIVIA

Since the FDIC was created in 1933, not a single depositor has lost even one cent in an FDIC insured bank.

each bank where you have an account. The maximum insurance for each depositor is scheduled to decrease in 2013 to $100,000, but the FDIC or the president can change that when the time comes.

How much money the bank pays you depends on the **interest rate**. The interest rate is the percentage a bank pays its customers for every dollar the customers keep in their accounts. Interest rates change a lot, depending on the situation in the country. In 1989, banks were paying about 9 percent interest on savings account; at the beginning of 2010, they were paying only about 1 percent. To explain how interest works, we're going to use 5 percent—a nice, round number. If the interest rate is 5 percent, the bank will pay you 5¢ a year for every dollar in your account. If you have $100 in your account, they pay you $5 a year. For $1,000, they will pay you $50 a year.

Your money keeps

growing this way. The bank keeps paying you interest on the money you deposit. If you leave that interest in your account, the bank will also pay you interest on the interest you have already earned. That is called **compound interest**.

Say your parents put $1,000 in a savings account for you. If the interest rate is 5 percent, at the end of the first year, your account will have about $1,050 in it—your original $1,000 plus an extra 5 percent, or $50.

If you leave your money there for another year, your account will have about $1,102.50 in it. In the second year, you earn $50 interest on your original deposit, *plus* another $2.50 interest on the interest you earned in the first year. After five years your bank account would earn a total of $276.28.

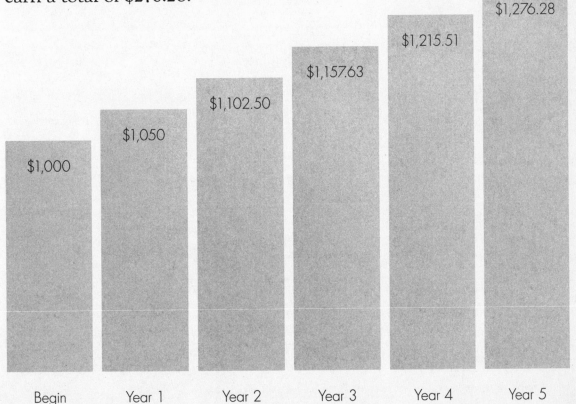

WHO SETS INTEREST RATES?

Interest rates are influenced by the Federal Reserve Bank, which is usually called the Fed. A special committee of the Fed (called the Federal Open Market Committee) meets eight times each year to plan how they want to affect two different kinds of interest rates.

The **discount rate** is the interest that banks have to pay if they want to borrow money directly from the Fed. The Fed is in charge of setting that rate. That rate, in turn, influences the **federal funds rate**, which is the rate that banks charge one another for overnight loans.

Why would banks have to borrow money? Suppose a large company wants to borrow a lot of money from a bank. The bank would be able to earn a lot of money from the interest it charges the company for that loan. But the bank cannot lend the money if they would not be left with enough cash to meet their reserve requirements. In that case, they would borrow money from another bank and pay it back as soon as they got more cash from other depositors.

Individual banks decide on the interest rates they are going to charge customers for the use of their money. The **prime rate** is the interest rate that each bank uses for its best customers, usually large companies. Other interest rates that the bank charges (including loans to smaller customers and the interest rates on their credit cards) are usually based on the prime rate, so those rates change as the prime rate changes. Below are some examples of average interest rates over a period of time.

1982: Fed Funds 12.25%, Mortgage 17%, Savings 12%

1989: Fed Funds 9.17%, Mortgage 11%, Savings 8.5%

1995: Fed Funds 5.9%, Mortgage 7.9%, Savings 4.75%, 1 Year CD 7%

2000: Fed Funds 6.42%, Mortgage 8.1%, Savings 5.5%, 1 Year CD 6.625%

2005: Fed Funds 3.33%, Mortgage 5.9%, Savings 2.35%, 1 Year CD 3.25%

2007: Fed Funds 5.04%, Mortgage 6.3%, Savings 4.25%, 1 Year CD 4.9%

2008: Fed Funds 1.85%, Mortgage 6%, Savings 2.5%, 1 Year CD 2.5%

2009: Fed Funds 0.25%, Mortgage 5.1%, Savings 0.5%, 1 Year CD 2%

DOUBLE YOUR MONEY

Here's a neat formula to figure out how long it will take you to double your money in a savings account.

> 72 ÷ interest rate = number of years to double your money

What does that mean?

Remember how we saw that at an interest rate of 5 percent, a deposit of $1,000 would be worth $1,276.28 in five years? Suppose you want to see how long it will take for that $1,000 to grow to $2,000. Easy! We just divide 72 by the interest rate (5) and get 14.4, or almost 14½ years.

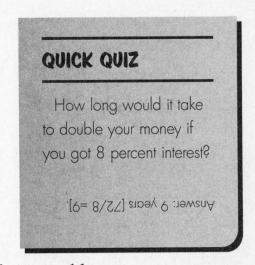

QUICK QUIZ

How long would it take to double your money if you got 8 percent interest?

Answer: 9 years [72/8 =9].

What do you think would happen if you could invest your money at 6 percent instead? We use the same rule: 72 divided by the interest rate (6) equals 12. So if you can find an interest rate that is only 1 percent higher, it will take 2½ fewer years to double your money!

As you can imagine, it takes a long time for money to double at the interest rates that savings banks usually pay. If you have $1,000 and your savings bank is paying 5 percent interest, you should think about whether it is worth waiting more than fourteen years to have $2,000. Remember those changes in prices that you found in Chapter One? Do you think $2,000 in fourteen years will buy as much as $1,000 will now?

HOW DO BANKS MAKE MONEY?

Banks would quickly go out of business if all they did was take deposits and pay interest on them. Banks need to make money to pay for their buildings, employees, telephones, electricity, and other services. Banks are also in business to make a **profit**.

Banks make money by combining the money from all of their depositors and lending that money to other people or companies. The customers of the bank who borrow the money are people who may want to buy cars or houses or go to college, and local businesses that may want to expand. When the banks lend money to these people and businesses, they charge interest on the loans.

If you were to borrow $1,000 from a bank for one year at an annual interest rate of 6 percent, at the end of the year you would have to pay back the original $1,000 plus 6 percent interest ($60). The total

HOW A BANK MAKES MONEY

Congratulations! You are the first person to call the radio station with the word of the day, and you win $5,000! You decide to put the money in the bank to save for college. The bank pays 1 percent interest on all deposits. At the end of one year, you will have $5050 in your account (your original $5,000 plus $50 interest).

The same day that you win the radio contest, Cousin Justin goes to the same bank and borrows $5,000 for one year to help him buy a new car. The bank is charging 6 percent interest on loans. At the end of the year, Cousin Justin has to pay the bank $5300.

The bank earned $300 in interest from Cousin Justin. It paid you $50 in interest on your deposit. The bank earned a profit of $250.

you would repay would be $1,060. The interest rate the bank charges for loans is always higher than the interest rate it pays for deposits.

We saw that when you deposit money in a savings account, the bank keeps paying you interest. When you borrow money from a bank, you keep paying the bank interest until the loan is paid. That interest can add up to a lot of money.

A SPECIAL KIND OF LOAN

One kind of loan that many people have experience with is a home mortgage.

Suppose you want to buy a house for $100,000. Most people can never save up enough money to pay that in cash. Banks and mortgage companies (the lenders) are there to help.

The people who want to buy the house (the borrowers) agree to pay a certain amount of cash right now. When we say the borrowers are "putting 20 percent down," it means that they are paying $20,000 (20 percent of $100,000) in cash and borrowing the remaining $80,000.

The lender is using a lot of its money to help the people buy their house. And the lender is charging interest on that money so it can make a big profit. But how does it know it will get its money back?

The lender doesn't know for certain, but it does have one advantage: If the borrowers stop making their mortgage payments, the lender can just take the house back and sell it to someone else. When that happens, we say that the lender has **foreclosed** on the house.

PUTTING YOUR MONEY IN A SAVINGS BANK

🐷 Before you select a bank for your savings account, compare the interest rates of all the banks in your neighborhood. Interest rates change often, but you will want to start with the highest rate you can.

🐷 Find out if you can get a higher rate of interest if you keep your money in a CD. Banks offer different choices of CDs with different rates of interest for different lengths of time. Consider what choice is best for you.

🐷 You should also think about whether the bank and its ATMs are convenient for you and your parents and whether you can mail in your deposits.

🐷 Some banks charge you a monthly fee if you keep less than a certain amount of money in your account. Be sure to ask about that before you open your account.

You need to have a parent with you to open a bank account. You and your parent can open the account by going into the nearest branch of the bank you select. You may also be able to open an account online.

If you want to know how much money you have or how much interest you have earned, the best thing to do is check out your account on the bank's website. That information will be much more up to date than the bank statement you receive in the mail. In fact, you can even choose to never get a paper statement in the mail, and just get all your information online.

Suppose you need to know your balance when you're not at a computer. No problem! If you got an ATM card when you opened your account, you can get that information at any of your bank's ATMs. Many banks will give you that information over the phone as well.

WHO SHOULD PUT MONEY IN A SAVINGS ACCOUNT?

The good things about savings accounts are that they are very safe and you can get your money easily if you need it.

Remember, you should never put all your eggs in one basket. Even risk lovers should put some money in a savings bank, especially if they are going to need some of the money soon. If you are saving money to buy holiday presents for friends or family, a bank account is a good choice. Risk avoiders may want to put a bigger portion of their money in a bank, but also may want to put some money in other, higher-risk investments, which may pay more.

CHAPTER FIVE

5 ALL ABOUT BONDS

Have you ever heard of Idealtown, USA? (If you have, write to us right away, because we thought we made it up just for this book!) Idealtown is the perfect place to live. The weather is great all year. There has never been a snowstorm, a hurricane, a flood, or an earthquake. The houses are nice and cozy, the streets are clean and safe, the schools are great, the stores are beautiful, and the neighbors are as friendly as can be.

Idealtown was a nice, well-kept secret for many years. Then, in 2010, some people from a big, famous magazine came to take pictures and write stories, and before anyone knew what happened, about two thousand new families decided to move to Idealtown.

The friendly Idealtown people were happy to have all these new neighbors. There were just a few small problems. With all those new families coming to Idealtown, they would need to build new schools, hire new teachers, expand the library and hospital, and maybe even build more playgrounds and soccer fields. Idealtown was happy to do these things, but where would they get the money?

The town needed $100 million to pay for everything the people wanted to do. They decided to borrow the money from investors by issuing bonds.

To borrow $100 million, Idealtown issued twenty thousand bonds for $5,000 each, with an interest rate of 6 percent and a **term** of twenty years. When Idealtown had to pay back the money it borrowed (in 2030), the bondholders would get back all of their original money ($5,000 for each bond they bought). While they held the bonds, the bondholders would receive 6 percent interest, or $300, each year for each bond they owned. At the end of the twenty years, each bondholder would have received $6,000 in interest for each bond!

$5,000 bond x 0.06 (6 percent interest) = $300 per year
$300 per year x 20 years = $6,000

When you invest in a bond, you may get a piece of paper that describes the details of the borrower's promises. When a person writes out a promise to pay back a loan, it is often called an IOU (a short way of saying "I Owe You"). The IOU from a city government, like Idealtown, is called a bond certificate. It tells you important things about the bond.

- **Face value** or **par**: the amount of money you will be paid back if you hold the bond until its **maturity date**

- **Maturity date**: the latest date by which the borrower must repay the loan
- **Coupon rate** or **yield**: the interest rate that the borrower is paying, based on the face value of the bond
- **Coupon payments**: how much will be paid at every interest period

April 1, 2011

I, Betty Borrower, do hereby promise that I will repay Suzie Saver $25 on June 1, 2011. Because Suzie is my best friend, she is not charging me any interest.

———————————————   ———————————————
Signature of Borrower   Signature of Lender

The bond expires on the maturity date. That is the date the loan must be repaid to you, the investor. The amount of time from the day the bond is issued to the day it expires is called the **term** of the bond. The term may be as long as thirty years (or more), but an investor can buy or sell the bonds at any time during the term. The person who owns the bond at the maturity date receives the face value for it. The person who sells the bond before its maturity date may receive more or less than its full, or face, value.

KINDS OF BONDS

When governments or companies need money, they cannot go to a bank for a loan the way an individual person can. Instead, they **issue** bonds to borrow the money they need. There are three different types of bonds, named according to the group that issues them. Companies issue **corporate bonds**, state and local governments issue municipal bonds, and the federal government issues treasury bonds.

Corporate bonds can be for any term. They usually have a higher interest rate than government bonds because they have a higher risk. People who lend money to companies can never be absolutely sure that they will get their money back. The company might not have enough money to pay back the loan when it is due. There's even a chance that the company might not still be in business by that time. In order to get people to take a chance on lending them money, companies have to offer higher interest rates than those offered by governments. Corporate bonds are usually issued in multiples of $1,000 or $5,000, and they pay interest to their investors every six months.

Municipal (state or local) bonds make interest payments every six months just like corporate bonds, but the interest rates they pay are usually lower than the ones paid by corporate bonds. So why would anyone want to buy municipal bonds? It's a little complicated to understand because it has to do with taxes, and you probably don't have to pay taxes right now. People have to pay taxes on the interest their money earns. That means they have to give the government some of that money. The good thing about municipal bonds is that there is no federal income tax on the interest earned from them. So because people get to keep more of the money they earn on municipal bonds, they are willing to earn a little less interest.

Treasury bonds are the bonds issued by the United States government and are usually considered to be the safest investments of all. We say that they are backed by "the full faith and **credit**" of our government, which means that we believe it is very, very unlikely that our government would not be able to pay back its loans.

The United States government has a few different ways of borrowing money:

- **Treasury notes (T-notes)** and **treasury bonds** are sold at their face value, just like corporate or municipal bonds, and you receive interest payments every six months. The only difference between the two is that T-notes mature in two, three, five, seven, or ten years, while treasury bonds mature in thirty years. The minimum purchase for either is $100, and you can buy them in multiples of $100.

- **Treasury Inflation-Protected Securities (TIPS)** are special bonds designed to protect you against inflation. The value of your bond is adjusted based on inflation, so if general prices go up, your bond is worth more. Then your interest is calculated based on the adjusted value of the bond. You still get your interest payments every six months, but the amount can change depending on whether prices have gone up or down since the last payment.

🐷 **Treasury bills (T-bills)** are short-term investments, ranging from four weeks to one year. The minimum purchase of a treasury bill is $100 and you can buy them in multiples of $100. Treasury bills work differently from the other kinds of bonds we've seen. You buy the bond at a discount, which means that you pay less than face value. So, for a $10,000 treasury bill, you might pay only $9,700. You do not receive interest every six months. But when you turn in the bond at its maturity date, you receive the $10,000 face value of the bond. So you've made $300. This "extra" $300 is really your interest. In this case, the total yield percentage would be 3.1 percent.

$300 ÷ $9,700 = 3.1 percent

🐷 **Savings bonds** earn interest for up to thirty years, and can be bought for as little as $25. If you own a savings bond, you cannot sell it to anyone else, but you can redeem it (cash it in) any time after one year, although you will pay a penalty for doing that.

TYPES OF SAVINGS BONDS

You may have some savings bonds that you received as gifts when you were born or for a special birthday. There are two different types of US savings bonds.

When you buy the paper version of the traditional Series EE US Savings Bonds, you pay half of the face value and redeem them for the full face value when they mature. The paper version comes in specific denominations, from $50 to $5,000. When you buy a Series EE Bond online, you can buy it for any amount you'd like, but you buy it for the full face value. When it matures, you get back the full face value plus all of the interest that it has earned. The term of the bond depends on the year in which it was purchased.

THE FIRST US BONDS

The first major bond issued in the United States was in 1790, when the government issued $80 million in bonds to help pay for the Revolutionary War debt.

Another type of US savings bond is the **Series I Bond**, which is also purchased at full face value with the interest added to that amount when it matures. When you buy the bond, there is a fixed interest rate that is guaranteed for thirty years. Then there is additional interest that is recalculated every six months, based on the rate of inflation.

HOW SAFE IS A BOND?

As far as investments go, most bonds are a good, safe bet. When you buy a bond, you know how much interest you will get. There is also a very, very good chance that you will get all of your money back if you keep the bond until its maturity date. Still, there are cases when the issuer (the government or company that borrowed your money) has business or financial problems and does not have the money to pay interest to the bondholders. When that happens, the borrower defaults. Every once in a while, the borrower does not have the money to pay back the original loan when it is due. Then the investor loses his original investment as well.

Treasury bonds are very safe. They are just about 100 percent guaranteed against default.

Municipal bonds are a little more risky. Although it is very rare, there have been times when a local government has not had enough money to pay the interest owed to the investors. Even when that has happened, the local government has almost always been able to fix its financial problems in time to pay back the money due on the maturity date of the municipal bond.

Corporate bonds can be safe or risky. If the company is very successful and looks like it will continue to be successful, there is almost no risk. The more financial problems the company is having, the greater the risk that it may not be able to pay back the money it borrows.

A VERY LONG-TERM INVESTMENT

In 1993, the Disney Corporation issued corporate bonds with a term of one hundred years. They mature in 2093!

WHO SHOULD BUY BONDS?

People who are more risk avoiders than risk lovers usually invest a lot of their money in bonds. They know just how much money they will get from the interest payments, how much the bond will be worth at maturity, and how long it will be until the bond matures.

Does that mean that bonds should be the only place to invest your money? No way. Can you guess why?

Besides the risk of default, another thing to think about when investing in bonds is inflation. When the bond matures, you get back all the money you paid for it. But that money may not be worth as much as when you bought the bond—even with all the interest money you received over the years.

Suppose you invest $10,000 in a thirty-year bond that will pay 6 percent interest. That means that you will get $600 every year for thirty years, for a total of $18,000. You will also get your $10,000 back, so you will have received $28,000 in total. Sounds pretty good, right? But remember, nobody knows what things will cost in the future. In 2010, you may be able to buy more stuff with $10,000 than you will be able to buy with $28,000 in 2040. So, is getting the same $600 a year every year for thirty years a good investment? No one can really answer that now!

If you hold your $10,000 bond until maturity, you will almost always get your $10,000 back. But suppose you don't want to wait until then. You can sell your bond to someone else, but you may not get as much money as you paid for it.

When you get $600 interest for your investment of $10,000, you are getting a return of 6 percent. What if the banks begin to offer higher interest rates before your thirty-year bond matures? Say the banks begin to offer 8 percent interest ten years after you buy your thirty-year bond. If you put your $10,000 in the bank then, you would earn $800 a year instead of only $600. Should you sell your bond and put the money in a bank? You can, but who would want to buy your bond? No one would want to get 6 percent interest with a bond when he or she could get 8 percent from the bank.

The biggest influence on the price at which you can sell your bond is the interest rate that other investors are paying. If people can get higher interest rates in other ways that are just as safe, they will not want to buy your bond. So the value of your bond will go down. Let's see how that works.

If someone were to buy your bond, he or she would want to get an 8 percent return on the investment, since that is what could be earned in a bank. Your $10,000 bond will pay the new owner $600 a year. How can the new owner be sure to get an 8 percent return?

Well, let's say he or she offers only $7,500 for the $10,000 bond. He or she will still get $600 a year in interest. That doesn't change. Six hundred dollars is 6 percent of $10,000, but it comes out to 8 percent of $7,500. Do the math and you'll see.

$$\$7,500 \times 0.08 = \$600$$

When the bond reaches maturity, the new owner will be repaid the original $10,000 from the company that issued the bond.

So, if you really needed the money you invested, you could sell your bond. But would you want to sell it for $2,500 less than you paid for it? It's important for you to remember that risk when you buy bonds that do not mature for a long time.

HOW DO YOU KNOW HOW RISKY A BOND IS?

Fortunately, it's easy to find out a bond's risk level. There are bond-rating services that do lots of research into all companies and governments that issue bonds. These companies give a rating to each bond. The rating indicates how likely it is that the borrower will not be able to pay back its loans. The higher the rating, the more likely the loans will be repaid. A rating of AAA is better than a rating of BBB.

Bonds with the lowest rating (BB or lower) are often called **junk bonds**. They are usually issued by companies that are facing a lot of financial problems. Sometimes these companies are able to hire new management, solve their problems, and pay back their loans. Sometimes they are not. Because these companies are very risky, they usually have to pay very high interest rates in order to get people to buy their bonds.

DO YOUR HOMEWORK

Before you buy a bond, be sure you check the **bond's rating** to get an idea of how safe the financial experts think that investment is. You can find out how a bond is rated by looking at reports in the library or on the Internet, or by calling your **broker** (if your family has one).

Two of the biggest and best-known bond-rating services are Moody's and Standard & Poor's. Here is how they rate bonds:

	MOODY'S	STANDARD & POOR'S
SUPER SAFE	Aaa	AAA
REALLY, REALLY SAFE	Aa1	AA+
	Aa2	AA
	Aa3	AA-
REALLY SAFE	A1	A+
	A2	A
	A3	A-
NOT VERY SAFE	Baa1	BBB+
	Baa2	BBB
	Baa3	BBB-
PRETTY RISKY	Ba1	BB+
	Ba2	BB
	Ba3	BB-
A LOT OF RISK	B1	B+
	B2	B
	B3	B-
VERY, VERY RISKY	Caa	CCC+
	—	CCC
	—	CCC-
IS, OR MAY BE, IN DEFAULT	Ca	—
	C	—
	—	D

BUYING BONDS

You can buy US treasury and savings bonds online at Treasury Direct or through a bank or broker. Other types of bonds (corporate and municipal) must be purchased through an investment salesperson or a financial advisor.

CHECKING ON YOUR BONDS

Since the interest that you receive on your bonds does not change, the only reason to check on them is if you want to sell them. The best way to check on the value of a bond is to look on the Internet or ask a broker.

SOME LAST WORDS ON BONDS

Even risk lovers sometimes buy bonds. If you know you will need your money soon, you may want to buy some low-risk, short-term bonds. You may not make as much money as you would with some other investments, but at least there is an excellent chance that you will get back all of your money when you need it. And always remember that it is a good policy to diversify. Even the most daredevil investors usually own some bonds.

THE FINANCIAL SUPER-MARKETS

You may not have noticed, but almost every newscast on TV or radio mentions something about the **stock market**. All day there are news reports about whether the stock market is up or down, if trading is heavy or light, and where the market closed for the day.

Why do the newspeople think it's so important to give us this information all day? For one thing, the stock market is a very important force in your life. You probably didn't realize this, but the stock market can affect what products are available for you to buy, how expensive the things you want will be, and even whether there will be jobs in the fields you want to work in when you graduate from school.

The second reason stock-market news is important to so many people is that almost half of the families in America have money invested in the stock market. Even cities, colleges, and banks invest in the stock market. Whether the stock market goes up or down may influence how soon your parents can retire, whether they can afford to send you to college, how much the college you want to attend can afford to grow, and many other things.

So if you want your money to try to make a lot *more* money for you, you'll need to know what the stock market is and how it works. The stock market is in the news so often that you may already know more than you realize. Let's begin with this short quiz. (The answers are at the end of the quiz, but try not to peek.)

Circle one answer for each question.

ARE YOU STOCK MARKET SAVVY?

1. Wall Street is:
    a) an expression that includes all buying and selling of stock.
    b) a place you go to buy stocks.
    c) a wall where a large billboard shows the price of every stock.
    d) all of the above.

2. You can find a stock exchange in:
    a) Tokyo.
    b) New York.
    c) Chicago.
    d) all of the above.

3. When you buy stock in a company, you are usually entitled to:

    a) vote on some of the decisions being made by the company.

    b) buy all of its products at half price.

    c) get a summer job at company headquarters.

    d) all of the above.

4. In order to buy stock, you must:

    a) go to Wall Street in New York City.

    b) own a computer and get on the Internet.

    c) be able to invest at least $20,000.

    d) be older than 18 or have your parents invest for you.

5. When people talk about how much risk there is in buying a stock, they mean:

    a) whether the company produces products that may be dangerous.

    b) how likely it is that you may lose some (or even all) of the money you invest.

    c) whether the president of the company likes to go skydiving.

    d) all of the above.

6. A broker is:

    a) anyone who has less money than you do.

    b) a person who does the actual buying and selling of stock for people.

    c) someone who decides the price for a stock.

    d) all of the above.

7. The price of a stock is determined by:

    a) a vote by all the shareholders of the stock.

    b) the US secretary of the Treasury.

    c) the people who want to buy and sell it.

    d) the president of the company.

8. To get information about a publicly traded company's financial history and outlook for the future, you need to:

   a) know someone who works there.

   b) read the *Wall Street Journal* every Monday.

   c) read the public reports the company has written.

   d) call a private detective because this information is not available to the public.

9. When you are selecting a stock to buy, it is very important to:

   a) be sure you like the letters it uses for its ticker symbol.

   b) ask everyone you meet if he or she has any "hot tips."

   c) look only at stocks that have very low prices.

   d) learn all you can about the company, its products, and its past performance.

10. The company's published reports may tell you:

   a) if they are being sued by anyone.

   b) their sales and costs for the past five years.

   c) the names of everyone on the board of directors.

   d) all of the above.

11. When you buy stock in a company, you are called a:

   a) director.

   b) lender.

   c) creditor.

   d) shareholder.

12. If the price of a stock went up last year, this year it will:

   a) increase again.

   b) go back down to its original price.

   c) stay the same for a year.

   d) increase, decrease, or stay the same—you can't tell from the information given.

13. It is usually considered best to buy stocks in:

a) only one industry, such as entertainment or computers.

b) companies with the youngest people on the board of directors.

c) several different industries.

d) only companies that have started in the last five years.

14. The price of a stock may change when there are big changes in:

a) the weather.

b) certain laws.

c) styles and fashions.

d) all of the above.

15. The executives of a company are:

a) not allowed to buy or sell stock in the company.

b) able to make more money on their stock because they know what is going to happen in the company.

c) allowed to buy stock in the company for half price.

d) required to announce publicly when they buy or sell stock in that company.

16. The easiest way to find out if the stock you bought has gone up or down in value is to:

a) look on the Internet.

b) ask your math teacher.

c) call the company.

d) wait until you get the next report from the company in the mail.

17. Companies are required to:

a) invite every shareholder to a meeting each year.

b) tell the shareholders how much they are paying top executives of the company.

c) report any possible good or bad news that might affect the price of the stock.

d) all of the above.

18. A company must send information about how it is doing to:
    a) everyone who owns more than five hundred shares of stock in the company.
    b) investment clubs that have at least ten members.
    c) teachers that have classes about the stock market.
    d) any person or company that owns at least one share of stock.

19. When a company shares profit with the people who own its stock, it is called a:
    a) bonus.
    b) reward.
    c) dividend.
    d) surprise.

20. Stock prices can change:
    a) at the three times a day set by the Treasury Department.
    b) every time a share of stock is sold.
    c) each morning, before the business day begins.
    d) every night, right before the day ends.

21. The P/E ratio for a company is the:
    a) percent of executives who take physical education at lunch.
    b) number of computers per employee.
    c) amount of peanut butter eaten in the cafeteria each week.
    d) price of the stock compared to the earnings of the company.

22. When you buy an "odd lot" of stock, you are buying:
    a) a number of shares that is not an even hundred.
    b) a number of shares that ends in an odd number.
    c) shares whose price per share is an odd number.
    d) shares in a strange company that does something no other company does.

23. When a company goes public, it:

    a) opens up company headquarters to the public for tours.

    b) issues stock that it sells to the general public.

    c) sends representatives out into the public to take opinion polls about its service.

    d) buys stock in other companies as an investment.

24. In 1960, the average annual income per person in the United States was about:

    a) $2,000.

    b) $5,000.

    c) $10,000.

    d) $20,000.

25. In 2008, the average annual income per person in the United States was about:

    a) $23,000.

    b) $34,000.

    c) $73,000.

    d) $100,000.

ANSWERS

1. A	8. C	15. D	22. A
2. D	9. D	16. A	23. B
3. A	10. D	17. D	24. A
4. D	11. D	18. D	25. B
5. B	12. D	19. C	
6. B	13. C	20. B	
7. C	14. D	21. D	

Okay . . . now, grade yourself. Count the number you got right, and rank yourself by the following scale.

25 correct: You may want to write your own book.

18–24 correct: You're on the money!

11–17 correct: You're no Wall Street whiz, but you know the basics.

3–9 correct: You are probably a wonderful person, but money matters aren't your strong suit.

0–2 correct: STOP! Read this book before you do anything else!

WHAT IS STOCK, ANYWAY?

Without issuing stock to the public, most of the big companies that produce the things that make our lives easy and enjoyable would not be here today.

Companies issue stock in order to get money to grow into bigger and better companies. Growing companies can develop new or improved products, manufacture more of the things we want, and invent better ways to make things. In addition, growing companies often create more jobs. When more people are working and earning money, there is more money to be spent, and other companies can grow as well. The entire country benefits.

Why would a company need more money to grow? Sometimes a small company suddenly finds that everyone wants to buy its products or services. Imagine a small electronics company that has invented a television that can transmit smells as well as pictures and sound. The owners of the company are sure that as soon as the first Smell-

E-Vision TVs are in stores, everyone will want to buy one. How will this small company be able to make enough new TVs to satisfy that many customers?

The company will need to buy machines to manufacture more Smell-E-Vision TVs and hire more people to run the machines. They will need to rent a bigger factory space and buy more trucks to deliver the TVs to stores around the country. They will need to hire a lot more people to drive the trucks, to take orders from customers, and to handle the money. They'll need money to do this.

One way a small company can get all this money is to issue bonds. Another way is to issue stock in the company. The people who buy the stock are called shareholders. Each shareholder owns a piece, or share, of the company.

If Smell-E-Vision, Inc., is successful, all of the shareholders will share the profits. Of course, there is a chance that customers won't really like to have all those smells in their homes. If it turns out that the idea stinks (ha-ha!) and the company is not successful, there will be no profits. No one will earn any money, and the shareholders may lose some or all of the money they invested!

Because people take a chance when they buy stock and invest money in a company, they usually have the right to vote on some important decisions, like who will be on the **board of directors** of the company.

Unlike when you buy bonds, when you buy stock, there is no promise that the company will pay you interest every year, and you may even lose the money you invested. So why would anyone want to buy stock? Because there is a chance you could make a lot of money if you pick the right stocks!

There are two ways you make money by investing in stock. One way is by receiving a share of the profits the company earns. Another way is by selling your shares of the stock to someone else for a higher price than you paid for those shares.

Why would a company want to issue stock instead of bonds? After all, if Smell-E-Vision, Inc., sells stock and is successful, it has to keep on sharing its profits and letting outside people vote on some decisions. That could really be a pain.

But, on the other hand, by issuing stock, the company does not create debt. If the company fails, there is no law requiring it to pay back the money it got from the investors.

The executives of Smell-E-Vision, Inc., may not want to issue bonds if they think they will not begin to make money for a long time. They still have to finish inventing the new TVs. Then they have to buy the equipment to manufacture them. After that, they have to produce thousands and thousands of Smell-E-Vision TVs, advertise them, find stores to sell them, and deliver them to the stores. The Smell-E-Vision executives do not want to have to worry about paying interest on bonds. They also realize that it may be a very long time before they have enough profit to pay back borrowed money. For Smell-E-Vision, Inc., issuing stock makes more sense than issuing bonds.

Let's look at how one imaginary company might use stock to raise the money it needs to get started.

PARTY-TIME PIZZA PALACE

Jennifer, Rachel, Allison, and Matthew had been friends as long as they could remember. When they graduated from college, they wanted to start a business together. One day, while eating at the only pizza place in town (the one that everyone always complained about), the friends realized that right there, in their town, there was a business opportunity.

They knew that before any business can even begin, the owners have to come up with a plan. They needed to decide:

🐷 what would be special about their business

🐷 where the business would be located

🐷 how much it would cost to start and run their business

🐷 where the start-up money would come from

The four friends decided that their restaurant would be in the mall. It would serve great pizza and super desserts, and it would be a fun place to go, with lots of things for kids to do. The next step was to begin to look at what they would need to get started and how much those things would cost. They would have to pay for:

🐷 location—deposit and the first month's rent for a space in the mall

🐷 furnishings and equipment—tables, chairs, plates, silverware, glasses, napkins, a dishwasher, pizza ovens, a refrigerator, a cash register, and computers

🐷 utilities—electricity, telephones, and other services

🐷 printing—checks, business cards, stationery, envelopes

🐷 advertising to get employees—cooks, waiters and waitresses, dishwashers, cashiers

🐷 more advertising to attract customers

🐷 salaries for employees

🐷 a lawyer to help set up the company and make sure the restaurant meets all the local legal requirements

🐷 an accountant to set up their bookkeeping and make sure they file their taxes correctly

They soon realized that there was going to be a lot of money going *out* before any customers or money would be coming *in*. They needed about $20,000 to open their business. The friends had $5,000 to start with. They needed to get another $15,000.

The group did not want to borrow money from relatives. They did not want to issue bonds or borrow money from a bank, either, because they did not want to have the extra expense of paying interest right away. So they decided to issue stock in their business. They looked for investors who would share some of the business risk with them.

The friends, who had named their business Party-Time Pizza Palace, were able to find three investors who would each invest $5,000 in their restaurant. That would give them the additional $15,000 they needed. When they added their own $5,000, they would have enough money to start their restaurant.

Investors in a business can be individuals, companies, or banks. For Party-Time Pizza Palace, there were four investors in all:

🐷 Party-Time Enterprises (the four friends themselves)

🐷 Jennifer's fourth-grade teacher, who always kept in touch with her

🐷 Matthew's old boss from his summer job at a day camp

🐷 the local Support Enterprise Club

PARTY-TIME ENTERPRISES	JENNIFER'S FOURTH-GRADE TEACHER	MATTHEW'S OLD BOSS	SUPPORT ENTERPRISE CLUB
$5,000 2,500 SHARES	$5,000 2,500 SHARES	$5,000 2,500 SHARES	$5,000 2,500 SHARES

In exchange for contributing money, each investor would own a portion of the business, or have **equity** in it.

Party-Time Pizza Palace issued 10,000 shares of stock. (They could have issued any number they wanted, but 10,000 is a nice, simple number to work with.) Since there were four equal investors, the 10,000 shares were divided into four equal parts. Each investor got 2,500 shares. Each share was worth $2.

$20,000 ÷ 10,000 shares = $2 per share

Party-Time Pizza Palace opened for business and turned out to be the hottest spot in town. Before they knew it, the friends found that every table was filled every night. They had a terrific take-out business, too. And soon every kid in town wanted to have a birthday party there. After only one year, the friends were able to pay all their bills and still had $14,000 profit to put in the bank!

The friends agreed that they would share some of the profit with their shareholders. They knew that they should not distribute *all* the profit they had made. They needed to save some of the money to keep the business going. The friends agreed that if the business continued to grow this way, they could afford to make a distribution to the stockholders of $10,000 a year.

Since there were 10,000 shares in the business, each share would earn $1 per year, or 25¢ each quarter (every three months). The money that a company sends to its shareholders each quarter is called a **dividend**. Every shareholder in Party-Time Pizza Palace would get a dividend of 25¢ every three months for each share owned. So, for 2,500 shares, a shareholder would receive a check for $625 each quarter.

25¢ per share x 2,500 shares = $625

The remainder of the profit, or **retained earnings**, was kept to help the business grow.

Party-Time Pizza Palace became such a hit that the friends decided to make improvements. They agreed to rent the space next door to enlarge their restaurant. They planned to redecorate the entire restaurant, buy two more pizza ovens, add more tables and chairs, hire more employees, put in video games, and add a room for laser tag. They needed a lot of money to do all that—much more than the retained earnings they had in the bank.

The friends decided the best way to raise all the **capital** they needed was to go public and invite anyone who wanted to buy stock to do so.

Going public is a very complicated process. A special kind of banker, called an **investment banker**, works with the company to issue the stock. The investment banker helps the owners of the company prepare all of the necessary forms and reports. The investment banker also helps the company figure out how much stock they can issue and what the price of each share should be.

The investment banker buys all of the stock that the company is issuing. Then, as quickly as possible, the investment banker tries to sell the stock to the general public.

When Party-Time Pizza Palace went public, the friends needed to raise $500,000. Because the business was so successful, the investment banker advised them to sell the new stock for $10 per share. They would need to sell 50,000 shares to get the money they needed.

50,000 shares x $10 = $500,000

The original investors who helped start the company (Jennifer's fourth-grade teacher, Matthew's old boss, the Support Enterprise Club, and the four friends themselves) were very excited. When the company was started, each investor had bought 2,500 shares for $2 per share. Each person's original $5,000 investment was now worth $25,000!

2,500 shares x $10 per share = $25,000

Jennifer's old teacher was so excited that she even bought more Party-Time stock. Party-Time Pizza Palace stock was soon listed on the Internet. The friends opened new restaurants in malls all over the state. The price of the stock went up to $30 per share, and the dividends doubled to 50¢ per share each quarter. Party-Time Pizza Palace became the biggest success story that town had ever seen!

NOT ALL BIG COMPANIES GO PUBLIC

Almost all of the famous companies you know are public companies, but there are some big companies that are privately held. One of those is the E. & J. Gallo Winery, which is still owned by the original Gallo family. Ernest Gallo and his brother Julio started the winery in 1933 with an investment of $5,900. Seventy-five years later, Gallo has become one of the largest wineries in the world, with sales of over one billion dollars. Ernest Gallo remained chief executive officer of the company until 2001. He retired at the age of ninety-one, and his son, Joseph E. Gallo, took over.

Have you ever worn Levi's jeans or jackets? Or Dockers slacks? Levi Strauss & Co. is another **privately held company** that makes these items. Levi Strauss started his company in 1853. In 1873, Mr. Strauss and his partner, Jacob Davis, filed the patent for the first riveted pocket blue jeans. Although Levi Strauss died in 1902, members of the Strauss family continued to control the company. In 1971, the family realized that they needed to make some changes and raise more money in order for the business to grow. Some of the company's shares were traded publicly until 1985, when the family bought back all the public shares and became a privately held company once again. Today, the company has more than eleven thousand employees and each year sells more than four billion dollars worth of products all over the world.

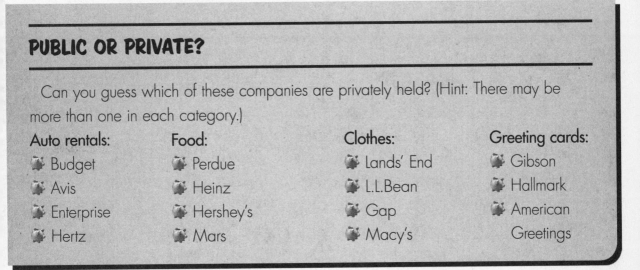

PUBLIC OR PRIVATE?

Can you guess which of these companies are privately held? (Hint: There may be more than one in each category.)

Auto rentals:	Food:	Clothes:	Greeting cards:
🐷 Budget	🐷 Perdue	🐷 Lands' End	🐷 Gibson
🐷 Avis	🐷 Heinz	🐷 L.L.Bean	🐷 Hallmark
🐷 Enterprise	🐷 Hershey's	🐷 Gap	🐷 American
🐷 Hertz	🐷 Mars	🐷 Macy's	Greetings

ANSWERS

The privately held companies are:

Auto rentals: **Enterprise**. Enterprise Rent-A-Car is the largest car rental company in North America. In fact, Enterprise Holdings also owns Alamo Rent A Car and National Car Rental. The company started in 1957 in the basement of a local Cadillac dealership next to the extremely noisy body shop. By 2010, Enterprise had almost a million vehicles in its rental fleet, and more than 68,000 employees in more than 7,000 locations worldwide. Andrew Taylor, the president and chief executive officer, is the son of founder Jack Taylor.

Food: **Perdue**. Back in 1917, Arthur Perdue had a nice job working for a railroad in eastern Maryland. One day he noticed that some people had sold a lot of chickens and eggs and were shipping them to customers in other parts of the country. Those people seemed to be doing very well financially, and Arthur Perdue decided that poultry was a good business to be in. By 1920, he was raising his own chickens and selling their eggs. Today, Perdue sells more than $4.6 billion of food and services in more than fifty countries. Arthur Perdue's grandson, Jim, is the chairman of the company, and Perdue's headquarters are across the road from the original chicken farm.

Mars (which also makes Uncle Ben's products, Whiskas and Sheba cat food, Snickers, M&M's, and other candies). Frank and Ethel Mars began making candy in 1911 and invented the Milky Way bar in 1923. When Frank Mars retired, his son, Forrest Mars Sr., (who invented M&M's) headed up the company. He was followed by his son, Forrest Mars Jr., and then by his grandchildren John and Jacqueline Mars. By 2010, the company was still owned by the Mars family, although an outsider had the top management position for the first time.

Clothes: **L.L.Bean**. Leon Leonwood Bean began his company in 1912 with the "Maine hunting shoe" that he invented. Today his company sells more than 16,000 different items. Since 2001, the chief executive officer has not been a member of the family, but the L.L.Bean company is still owned and controlled by Mr. Bean's descendents.

Greeting cards: **Hallmark**. Mr. Joyce C. Hall started his company in 1910 with two shoe boxes full of picture postcards. Mr. Hall died in 1982 at the age of ninety-one, but one hundred years after the company began, Joyce Hall's son, Donald J. Hall, was its chairman, and his grandsons, Donald Jr. and David Hall, played critical roles in the leadership of the company. In addition to greeting cards, Hallmark also produces Crayola Crayons and Silly Putty.

HOW TO BUY STOCK

In order to buy stock, you must be at least eighteen years old and you must open an account with a **stockbroker,** who will actually do the buying and selling for you. You can open an account by visiting the office of a stockbroker, by mail, by phone, or over the Internet.

STOCK CERTIFICATES

Until recently, public companies always gave each shareholder a **stock certificate** showing the number of shares that investor had purchased. The stock certificate proved that the person was the owner of that stock, and it had to be turned in when the stock was sold. You can imagine what a big job it must have been to keep track of all those paper certificates every time any stock was bought or sold! Today, all areas of investing have become computerized, and the information about the owner of the stock is kept electronically. If you want to have an actual stock certificate, you can usually ask for one, but you may have to pay a small extra fee. There are even a few companies that never issue stock certificates to anyone. When stock is privately held, as it was when Party-Time Pizza Palace first started up, the investor usually receives a stock certificate, but it is not very fancy or interesting to look at. There are stock certificates that are so cool-looking that some people actually make a hobby of collecting them.

CHAPTER SEVEN

7

BEHIND THE SCENES

The newscasts that report on the stock market often mention specific stocks. They may say, "Apple is up two points," or "Google is down three." What does that mean?

First of all, when we talk about stocks, each "point" represents $1. "Up" or "down" refers to a change in the price of the stock. Suppose that at the end of the business day on Tuesday, IBM sold for 115 (which means $115 per share), and at the end of the business day on Wednesday, it sold for 117 ($117 per share). The news reports would say, "IBM closed up two points." If you listen to the news several times a day, you'll hear that the price of a stock can change many times during the day.

Buying stock in a company is different from buying most other things. If you want to buy a book, a coat, or a candy bar, you look at the price tag to see how much it costs. The store or the manufacturer has decided on a price that they think is fair. You can choose whether or not you want to buy the item at that price. If you come back an hour later, it still will be the same price. Even a week later, it probably will be the same price. Sometimes, if you wait long enough, it may go on sale, but no one ever asks your opinion about the price.

Buying shares of stock is a very different situation. Buyers and sellers have equal say in determining what the final price of each share of a stock will be. The price is decided by an auction.

Have you ever seen an auction on TV or in the movies? Maybe you have read a newspaper article about an auction of a famous painting. If so, then you know that anyone at an auction may **bid** on the item. Each time someone makes an offer, the auctioneer gives everybody else a chance to make a higher offer. When it looks like no one wants to top the last offer, the auctioneer calls out, "Going, going . . . gone!" and the item is sold to the last (and highest) bidder.

Stocks are also sold in an auction, but there are so many stocks, and so many people who own stock, that it would be impossible to auction stocks in exactly the same way as a famous painting is auctioned.

People often talk about the stock market. They usually use that term to describe the whole business of buying and selling stocks, not one actual place or market.

News reports talk about **Wall Street**. In fact, there is a street in New York City called Wall Street, and it's right in the middle of Manhattan's financial district. In colonial days, there was actually a wall in this part of lower Manhattan, and it marked the northern boundary of the city. Today, though, the term "Wall Street" really refers to the entire business of investing. Many people who have jobs in this business say they "work on Wall Street" even though they may never actually go near that part of Manhattan.

So if "the stock market" and "Wall Street" are not where stocks are actually bought and sold, where does that happen? The place where most of the action takes place is called a **stock exchange**. The biggest physical stock exchange is the **New York Stock Exchange (NYSE)**, which includes NYSE Amex, the group that had formerly been the American Stock Exchange, in New York City. There are more than one hundred exchanges worldwide, and they are on every continent except Antarctica. The largest electronic stock exchange is the **Nasdaq** (National Association of Security Dealers Automated Quotations). Nasdaq stocks are traded over telephone and computer lines, not in a physical place.

Stocks are sold in a **two-way auction**, where many buyers bid on shares of stock and many sellers offer to sell stock at the same time. Of course, the people who actually own the stock don't have to go to the stock exchange themselves. There are brokers who represent the buyers and sellers and carry out their wishes.

In order for shares of a stock to be bought or sold, there must be a broker representing a buyer and a broker representing a seller. The buyer's broker says how much he is willing to pay for each share of stock. The seller's broker says how much he wants to receive. If the two brokers cannot agree, there will be no sale. Usually, they reach a compromise and the sale, or trade, is made.

Suppose, for example, you want to buy stock in Smell-E-Vision, Inc. You are willing to pay no more than $50 for each share. A person who owns one hundred shares of Smell-E-Vision, Inc., wants to sell his shares for no less than $60 per share. If neither of you changes your mind, the stock will not be sold.

If you really want to buy the stock, you may be willing to increase your offer to $55. The seller may be willing to reduce his asking price to $55. When the representatives of the buyer and seller agree on a price, they can make a deal and a sale can take place.

NEWS FLASH FROM THE PAST

The first stock exchange in the United States was established in Philadelphia in 1790. Investors in Philadelphia soon became worried that the investors in New York would have an unfair advantage. The New Yorkers got important business news first—as soon as the ships from Europe landed there.

Some Philadelphia brokers wanted to fix that problem. There were no telephones then, and even horses took a long time to make the trip between the two cities.

Finally, they stationed people on high points across New Jersey (which is between New York and Philadelphia) and set up a code of flashes of light that could relay stock prices and other news. This system worked so well that news could get all the way from New York to Philadelphia in as few as ten minutes!

WHAT MAKES THE PRICE OF STOCK CHANGE?

If many people think a company is going to make a lot of money, they all will want to own a share of that company. Just as in an auction for a famous painting, when many people want to buy the same stock, they keep offering higher bids for each share, and the price of the stock goes up. If a pharmaceutical company announces that it is close to finding a medicine to stop baldness, everyone will want to buy stock in that company.

Sometimes there is bad news that affects a company. Suppose an automobile company has to recall many of its cars because the air bags are not working correctly, and a few months later has to recall other cars because their headlights aren't working properly. Customers might not trust that company's cars and might not want to buy them in the future. Investors then would not be anxious to buy stock in that company, and the price of each share would go down.

STOCK FACTS

First listed corporate stock: Bank of New York, 1792

Longest listed stock: Con Edison, listed in 1824 as New York Gas Light Company

The price of any stock can change many times during a day. Every time someone wants to buy or sell shares of stock, the buyer and seller both must agree to the price before a trade can be made.

INSIDE THE NEW YORK STOCK EXCHANGE

The New York Stock Exchange (NYSE) began in 1792, when a group of twenty-four brokers and merchants began to meet under a buttonwood tree on Wall Street. Those brokers set up their own rules for trading and promised that they would always do business with one another rather than with "outsiders."

Some companies wanted to sell their stock, but they were not large enough to be listed on the New York Stock Exchange. So, in 1842, other brokers set up their own group to trade stocks in those smaller companies. Every day these brokers met on a curb outside the New York Stock Exchange. In 1921, they finally moved indoors to their own building. This group of brokers was called the New York Curb Exchange until 1953, when it changed its name to the American Stock Exchange.

ANOTHER WAY TO COMMUNICATE

The brokers who met outside had a hard time hearing one another above the noises of the wind, rain, and everyone else on the street. They solved this problem by developing a system of hand signals to communicate with one another and with their clerks who worked in offices nearby. Those hand signals worked so well that brokers continued to use them, even after they had moved indoors.

The first home of the New York Stock Exchange (in 1817) was in a rented room at 40 Wall Street. As more companies listed their stocks and more people became involved in trading stocks, more and more space was needed. The current Exchange building at 18 Broad Street opened in 1903 with one giant trading room.

As more companies became listed for trading, the NYSE had to expand to have enough room to trade all of those stocks. Eventually trading was conducted in five huge rooms, and about three thousand people worked on the floor of the Exchange to handle all the trades.

Like your family and your school, the NYSE uses technology that makes everything easier to do. In 1995, some floor brokers began to use wireless handheld computers, and by 2004 almost everyone was using one.

In 2006, the New York Stock Exchange **merged** with Archipelago, a company that specialized in systems that could trade stocks electronically. The following year, it merged with Euronext, a company that operated stock exchanges in five European countries, and the name of the organization became NYSE Euronext. Then in 2008, that company **acquired** the American Stock Exchange, which is now known as NYSE Amex.

Today, about 1,200 people work on the floor of the NYSE (about half as many as there were ten years ago), and all the trades are handled in just two rooms. All of that efficiency is possible because of technology.

The central part of each room of the Exchange is known as the **trading floor**. In the very center are the **trading posts**, where the actual buying and selling take place. Every stock is assigned to a specific trading post and is traded only at that post. Each of the trading posts has electronic signs right outside of it. These signs show every stock that is traded at that post, the current bid and offer for each stock, and the last sale and the net change for the day.

Around the outer edges of each room are **booths**. Each of the brokerage houses has its "headquarters" in one of the booths. Brokerage firms on the NYSE range from large recognizable names that provide full brokerage services to smaller independent firms that specialize solely in trading for large organizations.

STOCK EXCHANGE STYLES

Many people who work on the trading floor wear different colored jackets. Managers who work for the NYSE wear green jackets. Brokers and assistants often wear other colors that identify the companies they work for. Before automation came to the NYSE, messengers wore light blue jackets with orange shoulder epaulets and reporters wore navy jackets.

A DAY AT THE NEW YORK STOCK EXCHANGE

At 9:30 AM, a bell rings to let everyone know that the trading day has begun. Orders to buy and sell stock begin to come in from all over the country and all over the world. If you watch old movies of the New York Stock Exchange, you will see lots of people answering phones, writing notes on little pieces of papers, scurrying around like mad, and tossing those little papers wherever they please. Today, there's no need to do all that. Orders to buy or sell come in electronically. They may go straight to a trading post or they may go to the handheld computer of one of the brokers.

One of the orders might be from a stockbroker in your town, who is following your instructions to buy one hundred shares of Party-Time Pizza Palace stock. In the old days, a **floor broker** would take your order to the trading post where Party-Time's stock was traded. He would meet a floor broker from another **brokerage house** who had an order to sell shares of Party-Time Pizza Palace stock. The two brokers would find a price that was agreeable to both of them and the trade would be executed.

In the modern world, things happen much faster and more efficiently. Orders that come in directly to a trading post are executed automatically and immediately. Orders that come in to a floor broker may be passed on to the trading post or the broker may choose to execute the trade the old-fashioned way. Brokers can't do that for everyone, though. The average trade handled by a floor broker is for a large organization and is usually for twenty thousand shares or more.

After the stock is sold, the number of shares and the price per share are recorded in the exchange's electronic system and communicated to every broker on the floor, to all brokers across the country, and to every place where trading results are shown—the Internet, the bottom of your TV screen, and anyplace else you can think of.

Now that you are an owner of Party-Time Pizza Palace stock, you are registered as a shareholder in the company's computer. If you want to get a stock certificate, you can ask your stockbroker to send one to your home. You might want to keep your stock certificate in a **safe-deposit box** at your bank. Or you might even want to frame it in your room.

All day, the people on the floor of the exchange complete trades. The floor brokers are constantly using their handheld computers, where they can see the prices that stocks have traded at or how the overall market is doing. They can execute trades, fill out the forms that are needed to record those trades, send messages to one another or to brokers in other cities, and use some of the complex systems that help them know when to buy or sell different stocks. At the New York Stock Exchange, there are almost one and a half billion shares traded on an average day. (That's more than four million separate trades!) Fortunately, brokers no longer have to run to trading posts for every trade!

RECORD DAYS ON THE NYSE (AS OF 1/1/10)

| Slowest Day | March 31, 1830 | 31 shares traded |
| Busiest Day | December 18, 2009 | 3.16 billion shares traded |

CHAPTER EIGHT

8

MAKING MONEY IN THE STOCK MARKET

People invest in the stock market for one basic reason: to make money.

There are two ways to make money in the stock market. One way is by receiving dividends, or a share of the company's profits. The second way is to sell the stock to someone else at a higher price per share than what you paid for it.

Before you buy a stock, you can find out how much the company pays each year in dividends for each share. Dividends must be approved by the board of directors. Companies can change the amounts of their dividends whenever they want, but usually they change them only if business has been very good—or very bad.

People who want to receive regular payments should look at stocks with high dividend rates. Even if the amount of the dividend is not the main reason you are buying shares of a particular stock, you still should pay attention to changes in the dividend rates. Whenever a company declares its dividends, the announcement can affect the price of the stock.

If a company increases its dividend, investors believe that the management of the company has good reason to be optimistic about future profits. More investors will want to buy the stock, and the price will go up. If the company announces a smaller dividend, or says that there will be no dividend at all that quarter, it may look like the management is concerned about the company's future and does not want to commit itself to giving out high dividends. That kind of news can make the price of the stock go down.

If you are a risk avoider, you probably will want to invest only a small portion of your money in stocks. When you do buy stocks, you probably will prefer those that have a solid history of paying dividends. That way you will know in advance how much money you are likely to make from your investment each year. Also, stocks that pay high dividends are generally in well-established companies where there is less risk of losing money.

NO DIVIDENDS FROM THESE COMPANIES

Amazon and eBay do not pay dividends to their investors. Neither do DirectTV, Dell, or Apple (although Apple did pay dividends between 1987 and 1995).

Do you see anything these companies have in common? They are all Internet and technology oriented.

The other way people can make money in the stock market is to sell the stock when its price **appreciates,** or goes up. Risk lovers often buy shares of stock in new or small companies. If a new company does become successful, the value of its stock will increase and the investor can sell it for a profit. If the company does not become successful, the investor may lose part or all of his or her investment. Risk lovers accept that possibility because there is also a chance of making a lot of money if their predictions are correct. Companies whose stock may either increase or decrease a lot usually do not pay dividends to their shareholders. Instead, they keep all of their profits to use for their own growth. These companies are betting that they will become very profitable. When that happens, the shareholders will be able to make money because the price of the shares will go way up.

SPLITS

Sometimes a company announces a stock **split**. If the split is "two for one," you will get an additional share for each share you already own. The value of each share will be adjusted for the split so that you end up having the same amount of money invested in the company. If you had one hundred shares at $30 each, you now have two hundred shares at $15 each. Either way, you still have $300 worth of stock in the company.

It's like a pie. You can cut it into four big pieces or eight smaller pieces. Either way, the whole pie is always the same size. And the amount of pie you have is the same, whether you have one piece of the four-slice pie or two pieces of the eight-slice pie.

Companies may have stock splits for many different reasons. One reason for a stock split is that the price per share might be getting very high. Stocks are almost always sold in round lots (one hundred shares). When the price per share becomes very high, buying round lots is harder for people. A stock split would cut the price per share in half and make **round lots** more affordable.

SOMETHING TO THINK ABOUT

In 1965, when McDonald's first went public, their stock sold for about $22.50 per share. You could have bought one hundred shares for about $2,250.

By the end of 2008, that stock was worth about $4,600,000.

There were twelve stock splits in that time, and the original one hundred shares would have turned into 74,360 shares. If you kept those shares for all of 2009, you would have received $0.55 in dividends for each share: a cool total of $40,898!

NO SPLITS FOR US!

As of 2010, Google's management has remained committed to its decision to never have a stock split. Its stock has been as high as $700 (in 2007). That's pretty expensive, but there *is* a way for you to own a piece of Google. Just invest in a mutual fund that has Google stock in its portfolio!

SOME BIG SPLASHES

One company that didn't pay dividends for a long time is Microsoft. People who bought stock in Microsoft when it went public in 1986 have seen huge profits from the increase in the price of its stock. If you bought one share in 1986, you paid about $28 for it. By March of 1999, your investment would have grown into $12,825—in only thirteen years.

Remember, though, that companies like Microsoft are for people who like taking risks. In December of 2003, Microsoft stock went down, and your original investment would have been worth only $6,955. That's still a nice profit on your original investment of $28, but a lot less than you could have had in 1999—almost $6,000 less! And that's if you had purchased only one share in 1986!

Another thing to remember is that strong companies usually recover from downturns in the stock market. By November of 2007, your Microsoft shares would have gone up to $9,677. That's still about $3,000 less than if you had sold at the highest point, but almost $3,000 more than if you had sold at the lowest point.

If you had bought one thousand shares of Microsoft stock in 1986, here's what your investment would have been worth:

March 1986	$28,000
December 1987	$115,171
March 1999	$12,825,000
December 2000	$11,592,000
May 2001	$7,209,216
November 2007	$9,676,800
February 2010	$8,043,840

How calm do you think you would have been as you watched your investment gain and lose so much money? That's what it means to invest in high-risk stocks!

Sometimes there is a company that many people are excited about, and they can't wait for it to go public so that they can become investors. Google was one of those companies.

When Google was starting up, the founders didn't have much money. To get people to work for them and to stay with the company, they offered their employees stock in the company for as little as thirty cents a share. The employees continued to work hard to make Google a success. After all, if the company did go public and issue stock, they could make a lot of money themselves. On August 19, 2004, Google finally made its first public offering of stock. It sold 19.6 million shares at $85 per share and raised more than one and a half billion dollars. Some of those shares offered on the first day came from Google employees. In fact, it's been estimated that nine hundred new millionaires were created that day!

> Employee buys 12,000 shares at 30¢ each = $3,600
> Employee sells 12,000 shares at $85 each = $1,020,000
> Profit = $1,016,400

MUTUAL FUNDS: THE EASIER WAY

When investors buy stock, they rarely purchase just one single share. Most of the time they buy several shares in each company in which they are interested. When you look at the prices of stocks, you can see that buying many different ones can be quite expensive. You can also see how much work it would be to keep track of everything that is going on in each of these companies. It's nice to own stock and make money, but do you really want to spend your whole day doing it?

Very rich people can buy many, many different stocks. They can hire people to watch their stocks for them and learn all about the companies and industries they have invested in. That gives them a real advantage in investing.

Suppose you are not one of those very rich people. There is a way that you can invest just like they can! It's called a mutual fund.

WHAT IS A MUTUAL FUND?

Suppose your family wanted to buy a vacation house but didn't have enough money for one. If they had friends who also wanted to do the same thing, they could all put their money together and buy a house to share. Then, if they sold the house in the future, they could share the profit as well.

A mutual fund is a lot like that. You want to buy a lot of different investments, but you don't have enough money to do that. You, and a lot of other people, put money into a mutual fund. Then the mutual fund manager decides which stocks, bonds, and other investments to purchase with all the money. Everyone who put in money owns a share in the mutual fund and gets to share in the profits—or the losses.

By investing in a mutual fund, you can own stocks in more kinds of industries than you could on your own. There are many types of mutual funds. Some invest in only one area, like technology or medicine or construction. Others invest in international companies or companies that protect the environment. There are mutual funds that specialize in companies kids would know, and others that only invest in companies that help people. There are mutual funds for almost every type of investor you can imagine. In fact, in 2008, there were more than 8,000 funds to choose from.

Mutual fund sponsors (companies like Fidelity and Vanguard) have many different funds within them, and every fund is listed separately. Before you invest in a mutual fund, it is very important to do the same kind of research as you would for an individual stock. Look at how well the fund manager has done in the past. Look at what kinds of companies the fund invests in.

WHAT CAN CAUSE CHANGES IN THE PRICES OF STOCKS?

Of course, no one can really predict which stocks will increase or decrease. But there *are* a lot of good hints out there—you just have to know where to look for them. Here are some things to think about.

- **Laws:** If the government passes a law that people cannot buy cars that use a lot of gas and create a lot of pollution, the companies that produce those cars will make less money, and fewer people will want to own their stocks. The prices will go down. Companies that make nonpolluting cars will have better sales and earn more money. The high demand for their stocks will cause the price of each share to go up.

New discoveries: A medicine to cure the common cold would be great for most of us and for the drug company that sells the medicine. Its stock would go up. But what about the companies that make tissues, nasal sprays, and cough drops? People wouldn't need (or buy) their products as much, so the prices of their stocks might go down.

Weather: If there is a frost in Florida or California, there will be fewer oranges available. Companies that sell oranges or orange juice will not have enough to sell, and those companies will make less money. Their stocks might go down. On the other hand, a really bad, snowy winter would be good for the companies that make snowblowers, shovels, snow boots, skis, and snowplows. The prices of their stocks might go up.

Current events: Even terrible situations like war can have an influence on the price of stocks. Companies that make the equipment for tanks, guns, and fighter planes have more business when a country is at war. A natural tragedy, like a hurricane, can help the companies that sell the supplies people need to rebuild their homes and businesses. But if that hurricane strikes a place that tourists usually visit, it hurts the hotels, the restaurants, and the airlines that usually serve those tourists.

The general economy: When the country is doing well and companies are making good profits, they may hire more people and pay higher salaries. People may use their extra money to go on nice vacations, to buy bigger homes or redecorate the homes they have, or to buy clothes and jewelry. On the other hand, when things are not so good, a lot of people may be out of work or afraid of losing their jobs. When people are worried about making money, they try to spend as little as possible. That could mean lower profits for restaurants, movie theaters, clothing manufacturers, retail stores, car manufacturers and dealers, and vacation businesses. Businesses that sell things that are not true necessities will be hurt, and many will see their stock price go down.

🐷 **Negative publicity**: A news article about how some cosmetics companies test their products on animals might result in many people refusing to buy products from those companies. The stocks of those companies would go down.

🐷 **Trends and styles**: When many businesses decided that men no longer had to wear suits and ties to work, the companies that manufactured ties began to have lower profits. Other companies that produce sport shirts, sweaters, or casual pants looked forward to much greater sales and profits.

🐷 **Changes in the population**: People are living a lot longer than they used to. That means more sales for companies that manufacture things like hearing aids. If people begin to retire at an earlier age, there will be more sales of things like golf clubs and equipment for other leisure activities.

Changes in attitudes: For a long time, very few people cared about global warming and other environmental issues. When there is a lot of news about the importance of protecting the environment, companies that make things like solar heating panels or perform services like recycling are seen as extremely desirable, and their stock prices go up.

Investing in the stock market is never a safe bet. You can make a lot of money, but you also can lose a lot of money. Even extreme risk lovers should diversify their portfolios and include some "safer" stocks as well as bonds and other types of investments.

A FABLE

About a hundred years ago, when almost no one had a car, people would travel in carriages or buggies pulled by horses. There were many companies that made those buggies and the equipment for them. The company that made the very best equipment was Super Ultimate Buggies (known as SUB).

Back then, there was a fellow named Danny N. Vestor who wanted to invest his money. He bought one thousand shares of stock in SUB, and paid $20 for each share. He invested a total of $20,000.

Other investors also wanted to own SUB stock. People wanted it so much that a year after Danny bought his stock, buyers were offering to pay $30 for each share! Now Danny's investment of $20,000 was worth $30,000. Danny's mother thought it would be a good time to sell his stock, but Danny wanted to hang on to all his shares.

Unfortunately, Danny did not pay enough attention to the automobiles that had started to appear on the roads. He thought they were just a passing fad. Danny walked right past the empty buggy-supply stores and hardly gave them a second glance.

Five years later, Danny finally bought his family a car. That same day, he decided to sell his shares of Super Ultimate Buggy and buy stock in a car company instead.

Danny's broker had one small problem when he tried to sell the stock. Everyone else had already seen that there were fewer and fewer horse-drawn buggies on the roads. No one had to be a genius to realize that before long, buggies and buggy equipment would be gone, and SUB would be sunk.

Can you recall how stocks are sold? Remember the auction market, where the buyer and seller have to agree on the same price? Danny was a very willing seller. The problem was that no one wanted to buy his shares of SUB stock. The highest price he could get was $1 per share.

So Danny didn't listen to his mother. He didn't make $10,000 profit. Instead, this is what happened.

Bought 1,000 shares at $20 each   1,000 x $20 = $20,000 paid
Sold 1,000 shares at $1 each   1,000 x $1 = $1,000 received
$20,000 − $1,000 = $19,000 LOST!

Does this story make you think that it's crazy for anyone to buy stocks? Well, it isn't. In fact, over a long period of time, stocks have made more money than any other type of investment. On average, a person who invested $10 in stocks of small companies in 1926 would have had $143,000 in 2006! If that person had invested $10 in stocks from large companies, he would have had more than $34,000 in 2006. During those same eighty years, $10 invested in long-term government bonds would have grown to $800.

Stock prices did not keep increasing steadily throughout those eighty years. During that time, there were some very bad situations for investors. The worst was called the **Great Depression**. It began in 1929 and lasted through the late 1930s. The Great Depression was a time of terrible poverty all over America, when practically all businesses were struggling. In fact, if you bought stock just before the stock market crashed in October of 1929, you would have lost 80 percent of the money you invested.

So there are two very important words to consider when someone tells you about average increases over a period of time. One word is time; the other is average.

TIME

In eighty years, there have certainly been times when the prices of many stocks dropped a lot, but in general prices have always returned to where they were and then gone even higher. With most strong, well-established companies, if you can ride out the low points and hold on to your shares of stock for a long period of time, you will usually find they will recover from any drop in value and will be worth even more than before the drop.

What if you can't hold on to the stocks for a very long time? What if your college tuition bill is due or you suddenly need to buy a new computer? That's another risk in buying stock. If you need the money at a time when the stock market is at a low point, you can lose a great deal of money.

AVERAGE

Average refers to a group of numbers as a whole, not any one item in the group. You've seen this word often. If your math test scores are 98, 94, 96, 99, and 63 (on the one day you came down with the flu), your average for the year is 90. That doesn't mean that all of your scores (or any score) were 90. It doesn't even mean that all of your scores were passing.

It is true that, over time, stocks have increased a lot on average. But during that period there have been many stocks that have decreased a lot or even lost all of their value. And in the 1990s, when there were so many years of big profits in stocks, there were "blips," or brief downturns, in the stock market.

THE DOW JONES INDUSTRIAL AVERAGE

If you follow the stock market, either on television or online, you often hear about the **Dow Jones Industrial Average (the Dow)**. The Dow is a daily indication of how well the stock market is doing. It is established by taking the average price of thirty industrial **blue chip** stocks that are traded on the New York Stock Exchange.

On September 29, 2008, the Dow suffered its biggest point drop in history. The average price of the thirty stocks in the Dow Jones Industrial Average fell by 778 points, losing almost 7 percent of their total value in just one day. (The biggest percentage drop was on October 19, 1987, when the stocks in the Dow Average lost almost 23 percent of the value they had on the previous day.)

A big drop sometimes makes investors panic and rush to sell their stock. That's what happened in September of 2008. When stock prices started falling, many investors got nervous and tried to sell their stocks. Of course, they couldn't find anyone to bid very high prices for those stocks. Between September 15 and October 22 of that year, the Dow dropped 2,400 points and lost 22 percent of its value! When stock prices keep falling that way, we enter what is known as a **bear market**. (You'll find out more about this time period, sometimes called the Great Recession of 2008, on page 105.)

THE GREAT DEPRESSION

The worst day in the history of investing was Black Tuesday (October 29, 1929) when the stock market crashed. That day was one of the causes of the Great Depression.

The years before that had been great for most people. There were a lot of new things, like radios and cars, and most companies were growing like mad. During the 1920s, most people thought that stocks were a very safe investment, and investors were allowed to **buy on margin**. That meant that someone who wanted to buy $100 worth of stock could just pay $10 and his or her broker would lend the rest. That was a great deal and investors' money could double quickly.

Buy stock	$100
Pay	$10
Borrow	$90
Sell stock	$110
Pay back broker	$90
Keep	$20

Investor's money has doubled from $10 to $20.

A good deal, right? Until stock prices started falling. If the stock became worth only $80, the broker would issue a "margin call," and ask for the $90 the investor had borrowed. Oops—the investor didn't have that $90!

So everyone began to sell their stocks before they went down in value. Except what happens when everyone wants to sell and no one wants to buy? Right! The values go way, way down.

People were losing money because they had to sell their stocks for prices lower than they had paid for them. There were even some stocks that no one wanted to buy at all. Losing so much money that had been invested in stocks was very frightening. People were afraid that the banks would also fail and that they would lose that money, too, so they rushed down to the banks to withdraw their cash. A situation like that is known as a **bank run**.

Remember that banks lend out most of the money that is deposited in them, so they didn't have enough cash on hand to pay everyone who was lining up. More than nine thousand banks failed during the 1930s. And because there was no insurance on deposits in those days, many people lost all their savings.

When so many people lost all the money they had in stocks and in banks, no one could buy much. And when no one can afford to buy anything, companies make even less money and have to fire their workers. And then people have even *less* money to spend!

During this bad time, even the weather made things worse. There was a big drought, which meant that farmers weren't making money and there wasn't a lot of food.

The Dow Jones Industrial Average fell to its lowest point in the twentieth century. It didn't get back to where it had been for more than twenty-five years.

READING THE FINANCIAL NEWS

Do you realize how many products you use every day from companies whose stock you might want to buy? Are you aware that what you, your friends, and your family do every day can have an influence on the profits of those companies and the prices of their stocks?

Every time you buy something, you are helping that company make money. Let's take a look at some of the things you might do on a typical day. (The letters in parentheses are the **ticker symbol** for each stock.)

A DAY FULL OF STOCKS

When you shop for clothes, you may choose to spend your money at stores like JCPenney (JCP), Abercrombie & Fitch (ANF), Target (TGT), Guess (GES), or Gap (GPS). If you have a computer, it may be from Apple (AAPL), Dell (DELL), or HP (HPQ). Do you use your computer to get information from Google (GOOG) or Yahoo (YHOO)? Do you use it to buy books from Barnes & Noble (BKS) or Borders (BGP)?

Does your family have a cell phone provider? They may have chosen Verizon (VZ) or AT&T (T). Are the credit cards they use from Visa (V), MasterCard (MA), or American Express (AXP)? Even the food you eat, from Coke (KO) and Pepsi (PEP) to Burger King (BKC) and McDonald's (MCD), has an influence on the stock someone has invested in.

LEARNING ABOUT COMPANIES AND THEIR STOCK

There are many places to look for information about different companies. You can learn a lot from the financial or general news sections of newspapers, TV or radio news reports, the Internet, specialized newspapers and magazines, the company itself, and reports found in most public libraries.

BREAKING THE CODE: HOW TO READ THE FINANCIAL NEWS

The best place to find out about a stock is on the Internet. Most of the big search engines (like Google and Yahoo) as well as many of the largest newspapers (like the *New York Times*) give you information about companies and their stock. Most companies also share their financial information; you just have to know where to look. The best places to try on a company's website are the investor relations, corporate information, news, or press releases links.

Of course, all of that information doesn't help at all if it's in a language you don't understand. And investing information can definitely seem like a foreign language! Here are some of the most commonly used terms:

- **52 Wk High and Low**: The financial reports for each stock usually include the highest and lowest price for that stock during the past fifty-two weeks. There's often a graph to make the changes even more clear. That information is really important. For one thing, it shows you how volatile the stock is, which means how much its value has varied in a year. If the price goes up and down a lot, it might mean that the stock has a high risk, and that you might not want to invest in it if you know you need to have your money back on a certain date. Also, if the stock sold for a price that day that was higher than any price in the past fifty-two weeks (or lower than any price in the past fifty-two weeks), you would want to see if it is part of a general direction for the stock, or just something unusual for that day.

- **Stock**: The name of each company is abbreviated by a stock symbol. Party-Time Pizza Palace, for example, might be PPP. On the stock table you see that PPP (Party-Time Pizza Palace) sold for as much as $30 a share and for as little as $10 a share in the past fifty-two weeks.

- **Div**: This stands for "dividend." Remember, the dividend is the amount of money you can expect to get in a year for each share of stock you own. Companies that are newer and expect to grow a lot often pay very low dividends or none at all.

🐷 **Yld %:** This abbreviation stands for yield percentage. It tells you the amount of the dividend as a percentage of the stock's price. Yield percentage is a little like the interest rate for a savings account. If Party-Time Pizza Palace stock closed yesterday at $25 per share, and there is a dividend of $1 per year, the yield percentage would be 4 percent ($1 divided by $25 = 4 percent).

Because a stock's price changes all the time, so does the yield percentage. For example, if you buy shares in Zippy Sneakers for $50 a share, with a dividend of $5 per year, you are getting a yield of 10 percent (5 divided by 50 = 10 percent). If next week's listing shows a closing price of $75 a share and the same dividend of $5 per year, the yield percentage for people buying Zippy stock now will be only 6.7 percent (5 divided by 75 = 6.7 percent).

Remember: Your own yield percentage did not decrease, because it is based on what you paid, not what new investors are paying. As long as the dividend amount is the same, so is your yield percentage. And you've seen the price of each share you own go from $50 to $75. Nice going!

🐷 **P/E:** The price/earnings ratio is another way to evaluate a stock. The P/E is calculated by taking the price of a share and dividing it by the company's earnings per share.

Let's say that last year, a company earned profits of $6 million. All together, the company and investors owned one million shares of stock. So, the earnings per share was $6.00 ($6 million in earnings divided by one million shares = $6 per share).

Let's also say the stock is selling for $30 a share. So the P/E ratio is 5 ($30 price per share divided by $6 earnings per share = 5).

A high P/E number means that investors are willing to pay top dollar for the stock. Why would they want to do that? Because they believe that the company is going to be even more successful and have even higher earnings in the future.

What is a high P/E? There is no set number. Everything is relative. It's important for you to look at the P/E ratios for other companies in the same industry to see if the P/E ratio for the company you like has changed over the past few years. When the P/E ratio for a stock goes up, it means that investors have more confidence in that company now than they did before.

 Sales 100s: This tells you how many shares of that stock were traded. (To get the actual number, add two zeros to the number.) A letter z before the number indicates the actual number of shares traded, not in hundreds.

Sometimes the volume of trading in a stock is unusually high for a day. Heavy trading often is caused by a news report that mentions the company. If there is good news about the company, a lot of people will suddenly want to buy it, and the price will go up. If there is a bad news report, a lot of investors will want to sell, and the price may go down.

High/Low/Last: The highest, lowest, and last price the stock traded at during that day. These changes are not usually very large, unless there is major news about the company.

Net Change: The net change is the difference between the current price of the stock and the price at the end of the previous day's trading.

FY: Companies operate on what is known as a **fiscal year**. That means that their "year" is not necessarily from January to December. It can be any twelve-month period that they choose. You're probably familiar with this concept—when we're in school, we consider August or September to be the start of the new year. And for students and teachers, school years are never twelve months. Lucky us!

Market Capitalization: One way of judging the size of a company is by how much all of its stock is worth. To do that, we take the total number of shares that were issued and multiply that by the value of each share. Some people like to invest in "small cap" stocks, while others prefer "large cap."

SOME OTHER THINGS ON THE FINANCIAL SITES

When you look at the financial page for a company, you should also look at the performance of the whole group of stocks that it is part of. Financial sites usually show graphs of each of the major stock markets, as well as the Dow Jones Industrial Average. It's important to compare the stock you are considering to the bigger group. It may be a really good sign if your stock has increased in value by 5 percent. Or that may not be such a great sign if the whole market has increased by 10 percent.

Financial pages often show the major competitors of a company. That's another thing worth checking out.

Finally, many financial sites let you sign up for free alerts about a specific stock. That means that you can get automatic e-mails about how the stock is doing, so you don't have to remember to check on it all the time.

TRIVIA

In order to stay listed on the New York Stock Exchange, a company must have a minimum of $15 million market cap for at least thirty consecutive days. Looks like Party-Time Pizza Palace has quite a way to go!

CHAPTER TEN

10

BUYING AND SELLING STOCKS

Because you have to be eighteen in order to buy or sell stocks, your parents will have to place orders for you until you reach that age. There are a few different ways to buy or sell stocks. Full service brokers will execute your buy or sell orders. You can visit your broker in person, talk to him or her on the phone, or even send an e-mail. Full service brokers can also talk to you about your investment goals and give you advice about how to reach those goals.

Discount brokers may charge less for each trade, but they usually don't give you advice about what to buy or sell. Online brokers are usually divisions of larger brokerage houses. They usually charge very little to buy or sell stock, but they also do not give advice.

There are several different ways to place a buy or sell order. The most common is through **market orders**, which tell your broker to buy or sell the stock at whatever price it's currently trading.

You can also place a **stop order**, which lets you set the price for buying or selling your stock. For example, if Party-Time Pizza Palace is currently trading at $25 per share, and you put in a buy stop order for $20, then your broker will buy the stock for you when it drops to $20. If you put in a sell stop order for $30, then your broker will not sell it until the stock reaches a price of $30. A stop order is not a 100 percent guarantee. It's possible the price could change after your broker places the order for you.

TRIVIA

DRIPPING ALONG

Many companies have **Dividend Reinvestment Plans (DRIPs)**. When you sign up for a DRIP, your dividends are automatically put toward the purchase of more stock in the company. No brokers or broker fees are involved.

THE BULLS AND THE BEARS

In Chapter Eight, we learned about how things like laws, current events, trends and styles, and changes in the population can cause the price of some stocks to change.

Sometimes big events in the country or in the world might cause almost all stocks to increase or decease in value. A presidential election is one of those events. Right before an election, many people may not want to change their investments. They may be waiting to see who will be elected and how they think that person's ideas will influence the economy. Of course, there will be people who want to sell some of their stocks. When there are people who want to sell, and not many people who want to buy, the price of stocks may go down. After the election, most Americans tend to be excited about the new president. They think that their new leader will do things to help our country grow. So investors are willing to pay more for stocks, because they think that the companies they are buying stock in will become even more successful and more profitable. Then the whole stock market may go up in value.

During 1999 and 2000, the United States was in a **bull market**. Almost all stocks were increasing in value. Do you know why that happened? For one thing, many companies were making money, so people wanted to bid more for their stocks. Another reason for the bull market was the increase in value of all the stocks that were involved with the Internet and other technology businesses. Even though most of these companies were not making a profit, people thought that they would all become very profitable, and investors kept making higher bids for those stocks. When so many stocks were increasing in value so much, many people became very optimistic about the stock market, and kept investing more in it. Prices kept going up.

FACTS

BULL MARKETS get their name from the way bulls attack other animals: They charge with their heads down and then push UP with their horns to gore their target.

BEAR MARKETS are named for the way bears attack: They stand up tall and swipe DOWN with their paws.

Toward the end of 2000, we began to enter a bear market, and most stocks decreased in value. Why did that happen? One cause was that investors realized that the Internet companies were not going to be as profitable as they once thought. When that happened, those investors wanted to sell those stocks. But who would buy them? Only people who were willing to pay a lower price for them. And what happens when buyers want to pay a lower price? Right! Stock prices go down.

The bear market of the early 2000s continued to have an effect on our economy for a long time after that. When the average prices in the stock market were going down, people were not investing very much. They were not starting new companies or expanding existing ones. That was not a good situation because it is important for our country to continue to grow our economy—which just means producing, buying, and selling more things.

THE GREAT RECESSION OF 2008

You may have heard people talking about how times can be tough because of a recession. A recession is a period of at least six months in a row when the country's economy is declining instead of growing. Of course, there needs to be a way to measure that growth. Economists (people who study the economic situation) use something called the Gross Domestic Product, or GDP. The GDP is the total value of all the things that are produced in the country and all the services that were paid for. During a recession, many people lose their jobs, many factories close, and many families have a hard time paying their bills.

When the bear market at the beginning of the 2000s was causing the economy to slow down, the government lowered interest rates so that businesses would be able to borrow money and grow. When interest rates were very low, individual families decided to take advantage of the situation to buy homes. After all, everyone had seen how much houses could increase in value. From 2002 through 2005, interest rates were lower than they had been since the 1960s. It seemed like a great time to buy a home that you could sell later for a big profit.

It was a great plan—except for one thing. Many people didn't really have enough money for a down payment. Others had bad credit histories or weren't making enough money to pay even a low interest rate. So the banks made special deals with them. One thing the banks did was to offer subprime mortgages, which meant lending money to people who normally would not have qualified for such big loans. Another thing the banks did was offer adjustable rate mortgages that let borrowers start at a very low interest rate that would increase to a much higher rate in the future. Of course, the future eventually came, and those borrowers couldn't pay the higher rates. Do you remember what happens when people can't pay their mortgages? The bank forecloses and people lose their homes. And that wasn't the only problem. Home values did not keep going up as they had in the past. In fact, a lot of houses became worthless.

Remember our mortgage example of the family who put $20,000 down and borrowed $80,000 to buy their home? When house values started going down, a lot of those people found that they now owed $80,000 on a house that was only worth $60,000. So even if they could sell the house, they would still owe the lender another $20,000 and lose all of the cash they had put down in the beginning. A lot of people who found themselves in that situation decided to sell their houses at a loss.

The recession of 2008 affected almost everyone. In some ways, the economy is one big circle. When people can't pay their bills, they don't buy a lot of things. When companies can't sell a lot, they close factories and lay off workers. When there are more workers without jobs, there are more people who can't buy things.

By 2010, the government estimated that about 8.4 million jobs had disappeared. That meant there were a lot of people who didn't have money to spend. It also meant that there were a lot of people who weren't paying income taxes or sales taxes. And that meant that there was less money for governments to pay for things like schools and other services, and that governments needed even *more* money to pay for things that help people, like unemployment insurance and food stamps.

Some of the biggest banks also failed. Even though the banks could take back the homes of people who did not pay their mortgages, the banks could not sell those homes for the amount of money they were owed. And they weren't making money from the interest on new loans, either, because families were not borrowing to buy homes and businesses were not borrowing to grow.

The recession also affected the stock market. At the end of 2008, the Dow Jones Industrial Average lost 22 percent of its value! (If you don't remember why that happened, just flip back to page 92.)

WHOSE ADVICE SHOULD YOU TAKE?

There are so many places to look for information about stocks—in magazines, newsletters, and newspapers, and on TV, radio, and the Internet. It's really important to think about what advice you should listen to and what advice you should really ignore.

No one knows for sure what is going to happen to any stock. Most of the large brokerage firms have people who are experts at analyzing companies and making good guesses at what they think will happen to the stocks of those companies. Those analysts try their best to make good predictions.

There are also some individuals who try to predict what will happen to some companies. These people often post their opinions on Internet message boards or publish them in newsletters that look "official." Every once in a while, there is someone who does this in an illegal way in order to make money for himself.

How do people trick other investors? One trick is called "**pump and dump.**" People who want to manipulate stock (cause the value to change due to their actions) publish lots of things about a company that say how good it is. They might say that the company has a new invention, or has lots of orders for its products, or anything that might make it look like it's going to be very profitable. Other investors who see these predictions rush to buy the stock, and its price goes up. When the price is pumped up high enough, the manipulators dump, or sell, *their* stock and make a big profit. Because there was not a real reason for the price of the stock to be so high, the investors who bought the stock from the manipulators have no one to sell it to, and they lose all or most of their money.

It is illegal to manipulate the price of a stock. When manipulators are caught, they have to return any money they made, plus pay a big fine. They might also go to jail. But the worst part is that honest people who believed them have lost their money and can't get it back.

SOME OTHER WAYS INVESTORS CAN GET TRICKED

Although many investors have gotten tricked by "pump and dump" operations, some of the biggest scams of modern times depended on **insider trading** and **Ponzi schemes** to fool their victims. The people who ran the worst of these operations were so slick that

THE SEC PROTECTS INVESTORS

The **Securities and Exchange Commission (SEC)** protects investors in many ways. One of the rules for fair trading is that no one may have an unfair advantage to make more profit than somebody else.

Executives who work for a company usually know more than outside people about whether the company will be very successful (or much less successful). These executives are not allowed to use private information for their own advantage. In fact, the SEC is so concerned that everything is fair for all investors that absolutely no one can use private information for buying or selling stock in a company. That includes the people who print the company's reports, the husbands or wives of employees, and even the people who clean the company's offices.

even professional investment advisors got taken in by them. The SEC has changed many of its policies to try to prevent this in the future.

Insider Trading: When someone with privileged information uses it to buy and sell stocks, it is called insider trading. A company called Enron was involved in a very famous insider trading case in 2001. Enron was a company that made money by selling natural gas, electricity, and other products. Some of the executives found ways to make changes in the reports that the company had to submit to the shareholders and the SEC to make it look like the company was making more money than it actually was making. That made the stock increase in value, and the company encouraged its employees to buy its stock. The financial reports the company produced were so complicated that it took a long time for anyone to catch on. About twenty-nine of the top people in the company used their private insider information to sell their stock before it crashed when the truth about the reports came out. The very top person made about $67 million by selling his own stock. Eventually, everything became public and Enron went bankrupt. All of Enron's twenty-one thousand employees lost their jobs as well as every cent they had invested in Enron stock. All in all, the shareholders in Enron lost a total of eleven billion dollars! Some of the people involved in the cheating and insider trading were sent to jail for a very long time. But that didn't really help the people who lost their jobs and all the stock that they owned.

Ponzi Scheme: A Ponzi scheme is a way to make people think they are making money by paying old investors with money from new investors. For example: You take money from Mr. A to invest for him.

You keep part of that money for yourself, and when Mr. B gives you money to invest, you give some of it to Mr. A and let him think that money is his profit. You keep part of Mr. B's money, get more money from Mr. C, and tell Mr. B that part of *that* money is his profit. Most investors are so happy with their profits that they leave the money with you to keep investing for them.

The scheme was named for Charles Ponzi, who ran a huge scam in 1920. Ponzi did not invent this system, but he cheated so many people and took in so much money that he became known throughout the United States.

One of the biggest Ponzi schemes in history was run by a man named Bernard Madoff. Some of Mr. Madoff's investments were good ones and did make money for his clients, and he got to keep a little of that money as a **commission**. But after a while, Mr. Madoff got greedy and developed a fancy plan: a Ponzi scheme.

Mr. Madoff's scheme went on for a long time. The problems came when a lot of people wanted their investments and their profits and Mr. Madoff just didn't have it. He had already paid back some early investors, had paid for the costs of running his company, and had spent a huge amount on himself and his family. When he was caught in 2008, he admitted that his business was just a big Ponzi scheme. The people who gave him their money to invest lost about fifty billion dollars.

The people who were tricked by Mr. Madoff were not just

individual investors. Some of them were the people who managed the money for big organizations like colleges and charities. They got fooled because, like the managers at Enron, Mr. Madoff made his reports so complicated that not even extremely educated people could understand them.

COMMISSION

Commission is the money people are paid when they sell something for someone else. Many car salespeople work for commission in addition to their salaries. A salesperson who gets a 10 percent commission earns $2,000 every time he or she sells a $20,000 car.

PROTECT YOURSELF FROM STOCK SCAMS

- Never act on anyone's advice unless you can verify what he or she says through some other source.
- Never trust any newsletter that doesn't tell you who is sponsoring it or the names of its authors.
- Never believe any newsletter if it says it holds stock in any of the companies it recommends.
- Never invest in small, thinly traded companies unless you're willing to make a very, *very* risky investment.
- Never invest in something just because someone calls or e-mails you with a great deal or a "sure thing." Remember: If an offer sounds too good to be true, it probably isn't true.

CHAPTER *ELEVEN*

11

THE *GROWING MONEY* INVESTMENT GAME

Now for the really fun part—picking your investments and seeing how much money you can make.

You are going to be part of the *Growing Money* Investment Game. You may have played a different investment game in school, and it may have had different rules. The rules for the *Growing Money* Investment Game are in this chapter.

Of course, you will be using imaginary money, so we can afford to give you a lot to work with. We hereby give each reader of this book 10,000 *Growing Money* dollars.

You are going to pretend to invest this money. You will pick real investments and "buy" them at their real prices. You'll keep a record of the investments you "buy" and "sell," and at the end of six months you'll see how well you did.

You'll find personal record-keeping charts on page 129. If you and some friends want to see who can make the most profitable investments, just make copies of that page.

SOME RULES FOR OUR INVESTING GAME

1. Your Goal

You will start with $10,000. The goal is to see how much money you can make at the end of six months. You will play by the actual rules of real-life investing. If you buy a one-year bond, you cannot take that money out to use it for something else. If you buy a six-month treasury note, you must keep it for six months. You will also keep records of every investment you buy and sell and how much your portfolio is worth each month.

2. Allowable Investments

You may invest in savings banks, bonds, stocks, or mutual funds. Be sure to diversify among different kinds of investments. At least some of your portfolio should be in stock. You should not own more than four stocks at any time.

3. Interest and Dividends

Mark down the date you begin the game. If you have invested money in a savings account, you get interest at the end of every month. If you begin the game on the fifteenth of the month, you get interest on the fifteenth of every month. To calculate your interest, use one-twelfth of the annual interest rate that the bank is paying. For example: You have $2,000 in a savings account that is paying 5 percent interest; at the end of the first month, you get 0.417 percent interest, or $8.34.

5 percent ÷ 12 = 0.417 percent
0.417 percent of $2,000 = $8.34

Remember that at the end of the second month, your interest will be 0.417 percent of $2,008.33.

With bonds, you get half of the annual interest at the end of six months. For example: You bought a $5,000 bond that pays 6 percent interest. At the end of six months, you would get 3 percent interest, or $150.

6 percent ÷ 2 = 3 percent
3 percent of $5,000 = $150

Most bonds do not pay compound interest, as savings accounts do. At the end of the second six months, your interest would be 3 percent of $5,000, not 3 percent of $5,150.

If you have money invested in stocks that pay dividends, you receive one quarter of the annual dividend at the end of every three-month period. For example: You bought five hundred shares of a stock that pays an annual dividend of $2. Three months after you began the game, you receive dividends of $250.

$2 per year ÷ 4 = 50¢ every three months
50¢ per share times 500 shares = $250

4. Stock Prices to Use

When you buy or sell a stock, use the stock's closing price from the day before to determine the price at which you are buying or selling. You can get this information online.

5. Stock Selection

When you invest in stocks, consider those companies that make things or provide services that you know about and understand.

Now, all you have to do is . . .

BUY LOW, SELL HIGH

That's a famous expression about how to make money in the stock market. It means that when you invest in stocks, you should pick some good companies, buy each stock at a low price, and then sell it at a high price. Sounds easy, doesn't it?

Lots of things sound easy . . . until you try to do them. Then you see how complicated each step can be. Investing in the stock market is one of those things. It's easy to learn the basic concepts of wise investing. But then you have to understand more about those concepts, practice what you've learned, and have a little good luck, too.

When you play the *Growing Money* Investing Game, you will have to divide your $10,000 among different types of investments.

A moderate risk taker might decide to put $2,000 in a savings bank account, $5,000 in bonds, and $3,000 in a few different stocks. A risk lover might put $2,500 in bonds, $5,000 in two "safe stocks," and $2,500 in one riskier stock.

You've already learned how to make decisions about investing in savings accounts and different types of government or corporate bonds. Since one of the rules of the game is that you must invest some of your money in stocks, it's time to learn how to make decisions about buying and selling stock.

The basic steps in investing in stock sound very simple.

1. Pick the categories of stocks that you want to consider.
2. Pick three or four stocks you most want to invest in.
3. Buy shares in those companies when stock prices are low, and sell your shares when the prices are high.

PICK THE CATEGORIES OF STOCK YOU WANT TO LOOK AT

Another rule of this game is that you may buy stock only in companies that make products you know about. You will naturally pay more attention to those products and the things that affect them, so you will be able to make smarter investment choices.

The first thing you should do is identify some categories of companies. Take a look at the things you use or wear every day. Then think of the brands in those categories. For each one, write down your favorite brand, or the brand you think most people are using. For example, even though you may love your Dell computer, you may notice that most of

FAMOUS QUOTES FROM "EXPERTS"

"I think there is a world market for maybe five computers."
　　　—Thomas Watson, Chairman of IBM (1943)

"There is no reason anyone would want a computer in their home."
　　　—Ken Olson, president, chairman, founder of Digital Equipment Corp. (1977)

"640K ought to be enough for everybody."
　　　—Bill Gates, founder of Microsoft (1981)

"Everything that can be invented has been invented."
　　　—Charles H. Duell, Commissioner, US Office of Patents (1899)

"Who the hell wants to hear actors talk?"
　　　—H. M. Warner, founder of Warner Brothers (1927)

the people you know are using Apple computers. If people across the country are doing the same thing, Apple will make more profit and the price of its stock will go up. The opposite might happen to Dell.

To stay aware of what may influence the price of a stock, be sure to read the newspaper and watch the news on TV. But never forget that *you're the expert*. Even Warren Buffett, the successful investor, agrees that you can learn more, and sooner, from what you see in your local school, playground, or mall than you can just from watching the news.

It's important to watch and read the financial news, too. By the time a new medicine or invention gets reported in the regular news, investors already know about it. They have bought stock in that company, and the price has already increased.

As far as picking stocks is concerned, here are some categories to start with. We've included some ideas for each, but these ideas are just a beginning. Be sure to add any other companies that you can think of.

Categories I Know

Shoes (Crocs, Nike, Skechers) _____

_____

Toys (Mattel, Hasbro) _____

_____

Drug Stores (CVS, Rite Aid, Walgreens) _____

_____

Computers and Software (Apple, HP, Google, Microsoft, Yahoo)

_____

Food (Dole, Heinz, Kraft) _____

_____

Mass Market Stores (JCPenney, Target, WalMart) _____

_____

Specialized Stores (Office Depot, Staples, The Home Depot, Lowe's) _____

Fast Food (Burger King, McDonald's, Starbucks) _____

_____

Pizza (Domino's, California Pizza Kitchen, Papa John's) _____

_____

You probably can think of other categories you'd like to add. Remember that we are not making recommendations about the categories or companies mentioned. No one can predict what will happen by the time you read this book. We are only giving you some examples.

WHAT INFLUENCES HOW YOU PICK STOCKS?

Are there some issues that you really care about, like the environment or cancer research? Do you want to help by investing in companies that are working on those issues? Read newspapers, listen

SOMETIMES IT'S HARD TO FIND INFORMATION ABOUT A COMPANY YOU ARE INTERESTED IN BECAUSE IT IS REALLY A PART OF A BIGGER COMPANY. CAN YOU MATCH THESE STORES OR PRODUCTS WITH THE COMPANIES THEY ARE PART OF?

BlackBerry	PepsiCo
Hollister	Gap, Inc.
Old Navy	Procter & Gamble
Quaker Chewy Granola Bars	Dr Pepper
Taco Bell	Kraft Foods, Inc.
Snapple	The Coca-Cola Company
Iams	General Mills
Meow Mix Cat Food	Yum! Brands, Inc.
Minute Maid Orange Juice	Research In Motion
Oreo	Del Monte Foods
Betty Crocker	Abercrombie & Fitch

Answers: BlackBerry—Research In Motion, Hollister—Abercrombie & Fitch, Old Navy—Gap, Inc., Quaker Chewy Granola Bars—PepsiCo, Taco Bell—Yum! Brands, Inc., Snapple—Dr Pepper, Iams—Procter & Gamble, Meow Mix Cat Food—Del Monte Foods, Minute Maid Orange Juice—The Coca-Cola Company, Oreo—Kraft Foods Inc., Betty Crocker—General Mills to the radio, and watch the news on TV. Write down the companies that are doing important medical research or making products out of recycled materials. Maybe you would like to invest in companies that are in your state or that hire a lot of people from your town. On the flip side, there may be some companies that you want to avoid. If your parents have a car that has given them nothing but trouble, you may want to keep your money out of that company. What about companies that produce cigarettes, or have polluted a river in your state?

The Stocks I Want to Look At

INDUSTRY	STOCK	SYMBOL	EXCHANGE	PRICE	DIVIDEND	P/E

Now that you've picked some companies to consider investing in, the next step is to look at how the company has been doing for the past few years. People usually think that winners will keep winning.

If you hear about a teacher in the next grade who is supposed to be great, you really hope you will be in her class next year. You expect that she will be great again.

But suppose the Yankees win the next World Series. Lots of Yankees fans will expect them to be winners the year after, too. Sometimes they are; sometimes they aren't. A lot of things can change between seasons. There may be injuries or a change in players. Other teams may get some great new players, or just catch a couple of lucky breaks.

A successful company is a little like a team. With good managers and good products, it is likely to make profits. But if other competing companies start to make the same products—only better or cheaper— or hire the best managers, the original company may start to have troubles. To evaluate a company, you have to look at how it is doing today and also how it has done over the past few years.

On the other hand, don't depend totally on the company's history. Successful investor Warren Buffett once said, "If past history was all there was to the game, the list of the richest people would be librarians."

Believe it or not, anyone can get lots of information about any major company. Public companies (companies that sell their stock to anyone who wants to buy it) are not allowed to keep secrets. The best way to find out the history of the company is to get their **annual report**. There are three ways to do that: Go to the library, call the company, or look on the Internet.

The annual report will show you the financial history of the company for the past five years. Some important things to look at are: Has the company been taking in more money every year (has **revenue** increased)? Have there been big changes in expenses in the last five years? What has happened to profit?

Sometimes there is an increase in profit because the company has taken in more revenue. That is a sign of a strong company that is likely to keep growing. Sometimes a company can increase its profits by reducing expenses. Maybe the company closed a factory or bought less expensive materials. If the revenue is also not going up, there is not much chance that the company will grow. No company can keep reducing expenses forever.

The annual report will also explain any major changes that do not result from the regular business of the company. Perhaps the company shows a very low profit this year (or even a loss). That can be bad news or good news. The bad news would be that its products aren't selling very well anymore. The good news would be that the company spent a lot of money to buy another company that will help make them even more profitable in the future. For example, a company that prints newspapers may have a lot of equipment that they use only late at night and in the very early morning to print the morning papers. If they bought a company that prints catalogs, they could use the same printing equipment in the afternoon for the catalogs.

The new, bigger company could make more money than the two small companies put together. Here are a few reasons.

- When they were separate companies, they had two sets of equipment, and each was used only part of the time. They can save money by having only one set of equipment.
- They need only one building and warehouse.
- They will be buying more paper now, so they may get a cheaper price.
- They may need only one computer system.

Some other things to look for in the annual report:

- What does the annual report have to say about the competition? Is there one strong company that has most of the business in this industry, or are there a lot of small companies?
- What does the company forecast as its growth rate for the next five years?
- What else does the company do? How big a part of their business are the products you are interested in? You may find that a company that makes cookies also makes cigarettes. Or that film and camera sales are only a tiny piece of a company that makes office copiers and X-ray equipment.
- Are there any unusual circumstances? Is there any legal action against the company? Does the company have to spend a lot of money to meet new environmental requirements? Public companies must tell you about these things and estimate how much they might cost.

PICK THE STOCKS YOU WANT TO BUY

Now that you've looked at a lot of different stocks, you need to pick the top three or four that you want to buy. Many financial advisors think that these are the most important rules to follow:

- 🐷 Look for companies that have been around for a long time and that have had pretty steady growth. A new company with a hot product may be making a lot of money today but may disappear when the current fad is over.

- 🐷 Remember that even when you buy stock in a company that looks really safe, there is always some risk. The American car companies thought they ruled the world until about 1975. For many, many years, everyone thought those companies were very low risk. Then some Japanese companies (like Honda and Toyota) began to make cars that people wanted, and the stocks of some American car companies began to lose value.

- 🐷 Use your own common sense. Remember, you're the expert in what you see around you. Look at

WHAT DO YOU THINK?

The annual report for Suits and Boots clothing stores shows higher revenue this year than last year. Their **expenses** for manufacturing their suits and boots did not increase. The annual report also says that the company sold fewer suits and fewer boots than they did last year. How can this be? Does it show that the company is strong and growing?

Answer: They just increased the price of each item. They cannot keep growing if they keep selling less of their product and just keep charging more for it.

what people are doing in your school, on TV, and in the mall. If Speedy Burgers is always crowded, while Billy's Burgers is usually empty, you have some good clues about whose stock will grow more.

🍀 Don't put all your eggs in one basket—you should diversify when you buy stocks. If you buy stocks in different kinds of industries, you have less risk. It is not likely that there will be major problems in clothing, automobiles, restaurants, cereals, and airlines all at the same time. By diversifying, you give yourself a safety net. If one investment goes bad, at least your others may do well.

NARROWING THE CHOICES

Go back to your worksheet on page 121. Pick the stocks you most want to invest in. List them here.

_____
_____
_____
_____
_____
_____
_____
_____
_____
_____
_____

DECIDING WHEN TO SELL A STOCK

The important thing now is to keep track of your investments. You might want to take action if the price of your stock changes. This is the really hard part. Many people think that buying stock is simple compared to knowing when to sell. Do you remember the example of Microsoft in Chapter Eight? In that example, if you bought one thousand shares of that stock in 1986, you could have sold it for $12.8 million in 1999. If you held on to it until 2010, you could have sold it for $8 million . . . a difference of $4.8 million!

If the price of one of your stocks goes down, you may want to sell it so that you don't lose any more money. On the other hand, you may actually want to buy more!

EXAMPLE

Event	Cost
You buy twenty shares of Party-Time Pizza Palace stock at $80 per share.	$1,600
PPP stock drops to $60. You know that the company is still solid and will rebound. You buy twenty shares at $60.	$1,200

You now own forty shares.
In total, you paid $2,800 ($1,600 + $1,200).
Your average price per share is $70.
Even though you bought some shares for $80, you will still make a profit if the stock goes back up from $60 to $75, because you bought it at an average price of $70!

WHAT HAPPENS NOW?

To buy stock, bonds, or open a savings account or CD, all you have to do is fill in the Investment Tracking Records. Select whatever investments you want, as long as you follow the rules of the game, and do not spend more than $10,000.

You now own a collection of investments. This collection is called a portfolio. After all the research and decision making you went through to create this portfolio, it's tempting just to relax and come back in a few years to check it out. Not so fast!

Whatever you invest in, it's important for you to watch your investments to see which you want to keep and which you want to change. Try to keep a record of the performance of each of your investments. (Remember that gains and losses on stock are only "paper" numbers until you sell the stock.)

Once you have completed your portfolio, try to keep a record of your gains and losses for at least six months. You might check on your investments once or twice a week, or, if you get hooked, you might find yourself checking every day. Think about which of your stocks, bonds, and/or funds do well, and try to figure out why that is so. Likewise for the duds. It might be a good idea for you to start a folder for newspaper clippings concerning the companies and industries in which you've invested. That way, not only will you understand why prices are rising or falling, but you'll be able to make informed decisions when it comes time to buy or sell.

Remember, even though investing can sometimes be a gamble, learning the ropes now will help you handle your money wisely in the future. Good luck!

INVESTMENT TRACKING RECORDS

My Stocks

DATE	STOCK	SYMBOL	# SHARES	COST/SHARE	TOTAL COST	CURRENT PRICE/SHARE	CURRENT VALUE	"GAIN OR LOSS"

Value of My Portfolio

DATE	BALANCE	INVESTMENT	COST (MONEY SPENT)	MONEY RECEIVED	NEW BALANCE
3/4/10	$10,000	Savings Account	$2,000		$8,000
6/4/10	$8,000	Interest		$80.00	$8,080

GLOSSARY

Acquisition: the process by which one company buys most or all of the shares of another company in order to take control of it.

Annual report: a report that publicly held companies are required to issue each year. The annual report includes all of the company's activities and financial information for the past year compared to previous years and explanations of any major changes that did not result from the regular business of the company.

Appreciation: an increase in the value of an asset over time. The opposite of *depreciation*.

Ask: the price at which a seller is willing to sell a security; also known as the **offer price**. It usually includes the number of shares the seller is willing to sell at that price. The opposite of *bid*.

Asset: something that has value to a person or company. Assets can include stocks, bonds, real estate, or raw materials, such as oil, gold, or silver.

Average: the mathematical number that represents what is typical for a group of numbers, balancing out the highs and lows.

Bank run: a situation in which many people try to withdraw all of their money from a bank at the same time because they are afraid that the bank will not have enough money to return their deposits. Since the creation of the FDIC, bank runs no longer happen.

Bear market: a period during which prices of most investments decline, usually for a period of at least two months.

Bid: the price an investor is willing to pay for a security. It usually includes the number of shares the investor wants to buy. The opposite of *ask*.

Blue chips: the largest, most well established, most consistently profitable companies.

Board of directors: a group that is elected or appointed to approve all major decisions of a company. It usually hires (or fires) the top-level managers of the company and may have legal responsibility for corporate activities.

Bonds: a way for companies or governments to borrow money. Bonds usually specify when the lender will be repaid and how much interest will be paid to the lender.

Bond rating: an estimate made by financial experts of how likely it is that the borrower will be able to make interest payments and pay back the money borrowed on time.

Booths: workspaces around the outer edge of an exchange's trading floor where member firms and independent brokers receive orders.

Broker: a person who handles customer orders to buy and sell securities.

Brokerage house: a company that employs stockbrokers to make trades for investors.

Bull market: a period during which there is a steady increase in stock prices.

Buying on margin: purchasing stock by paying for a portion of it and borrowing the rest from a bank or broker.

Capital: the cash that a company has available to it.

Certificate of deposit (CD): an agreement with a bank to leave money deposited there for a specific interest rate and length of time. In exchange for that promise, the bank pays a higher interest rate than it does for regular savings accounts.

Commission: the money a person is paid to buy or sell something for someone else.

Compound interest: money that is paid on the original amount invested and also on any interest that has already been earned.

Corporate bond: a way for companies to raise money by borrowing from investors. Corporate bonds usually have a higher interest rate than government bonds because they have a higher risk.

Coupon payment: the amount of interest on a bond that is paid at each interest period.

Coupon rate or **Yield**: the interest rate that the borrower is paying on a bond, based on the bond's face value.

Credit: the amount of money that a person or company is able to borrow.

Discount rate: the interest rate that banks pay to borrow money from a Federal Reserve Bank.

Diversification: a way for investors to lower their risk by choosing different types of investments.

Dividend: a portion of a company's profits that is distributed to its shareholders, usually quarterly.

Dividend Reinvestment Plan (DRIP): an investment plan in which dividends are automatically put toward the purchase of more stock in the company. No brokers or broker fees are involved.

Dow Jones Industrial Average (the Dow): an average of thirty blue-chip stocks that is used as a daily indication of how well the stock market is doing.

Equity: in the stock market, ownership in a corporation in the form of stock; in a home, the difference between the mortgage and the value of the home.

Expenses: the things that a company has to pay for in order to get revenue. Expenses can include salaries, rent, or the materials to make the things the company sells.

Face value or **Par**: the amount of money that will be paid to an investor when a bond matures.

Federal Deposit Insurance Corporation (FDIC): a federal agency that insures that depositors will not lose their money in a member bank if the bank fails.

Federal funds rate: the overnight interest rate that banks charge when they lend to one another.

Fiscal year: the twelve-month period a company chooses to use for its financial reporting. It is not necessarily the same as a calendar year.

Floor broker: a person who makes the actual trades for people or companies on the floor of the stock exchange. They may be house brokers (employed by a brokerage house) or independent brokers (employed by a company that helps house brokers or other large traders).

Foreclosure: the process by which a lender can take ownership of a house if the borrower stops making mortgage payments.

Going public: the process of changing from a private company owned by a few people to a public company owned by many investors.

The Great Depression: the period between 1929 and the late 1930s during which many people lost all of their investments, unemployment was very high, and practically all businesses were struggling.

Growth stock: stock in a company whose earnings are growing faster than average. Growth stocks usually pay little or no dividends because they reinvest all of their profits in order to grow.

Income stock: a stock offering dividends that are higher than average.

Inflation: the general increase in the cost of everything, from cars and houses to burgers and fries.

Insider trading: the illegal purchase or sale of stock by someone who has knowledge about the company that is not available to the public, and therefore has an advantage over others.

Interest: the fee paid for the use of money. Borrowers pay interest; lenders earn interest.

Interest rate: the rate of interest paid as a percentage of the **principal**.

Investment banker: a special kind of banker who works with a company to issue its stock.

Investor: an individual or organization who gets paid for the use of their money.

Issue: the process of selling stocks or bonds to the public.

Junk bond: a bond with a low rating. Issuers of junk bonds often pay a high interest rate because there is a high risk that they may not be able to pay back the money that they borrowed.

Liquidity: the ability of an investment to be sold or converted back into cash very quickly and easily.

Market order: an instruction from investor to broker to buy or sell stock immediately at the best current price.

Maturity date: the date that money borrowed for a bond is due to be repaid.

Merger: a process in which two companies are combined into one.

Municipal bond: a way for counties, cities, and states to borrow money to pay for local improvements, such as roads, schools, and hospitals.

Mutual funds: an investment that allows many small investors to combine their funds so they can buy and sell a variety of stocks and/or bonds. Mutual funds also give small investors the advantage of professional management.

Nasdaq: previously an acronym for National Association of Security

Dealers Automated Quotations, it is a system that allows brokers to buy and sell stocks through telephone and computer networks rather than in a physical place.

New York Stock Exchange (NYSE): the oldest and largest physical stock exchange in the United States. It is located on Wall Street in New York City and is part of the NYSE Euronext.

Odd lot: a purchase or sale of stocks that is not a round lot (an even number of hundreds) of shares.

Offer price: the amount a seller is willing to accept for each share of stock; also known as *ask*.

Ponzi scheme: an illegal investment scam that lets people think they are making money by paying old investors with money from new investors.

Portfolio: a collection of investments all owned by the same person or organization.

Prime rate: the interest rate that banks charge their best customers, usually large companies.

Principal: the amount invested in a stock or the amount that is still owed on a bond.

Privately held company: a company whose shares are not bought or sold on public exchanges. A private company may have stock and shareholders, but it does not have to follow SEC regulations.

Profit: the money a company earns, equal to revenue minus expenses.

Publicly traded company: a company that has issued shares of stock that are traded on at least one stock exchange.

Pump and dump: an illegal way to make money in the stock market by manipulating the price of a stock to rise and then selling shares at a higher price.

Retained earnings: the portion of the profit a company keeps after paying dividends and taxes.

Revenue: the amount of money a company receives for its products or services before costs are deducted; also known as *income*.

Risk: the chance that the profit on an investment will be less than anticipated. Risk includes the chance of losing some or all of the original investment.

Round lot: the normal unit of sale for an item. For eggs, it is one dozen; for stocks, it is one hundred shares.

Safe-deposit box: a very safe box, usually in a bank's vault, which is rented to customers to store their valuables.

Savings bond: an investment that lends money to the federal government for a predetermined rate of interest and number of years. It cannot be sold to anyone else.

Securities and Exchange Commission (SEC): a federal agency that protects investors by setting and enforcing rules. Buying on margin, insider trading, and the reports that companies have to issue to shareholders are among the many things the SEC regulates.

Security: an investment that represents ownership (stock) or a loan (bond) to a corporation or government.

Series I Bond: a type of US savings bond that pays interest based on a fixed interest rate (established when the bond was purchased) and a variable rate that can change with inflation every six months.

Shareholder: a person or corporation who owns stock in a company or a mutual fund.

Split: a decision by a corporation to multiply the number of outstanding shares. The price of each share is adjusted so that each shareholder's investment is the same as it was before the split.

Stock: an investment that represents a portion, or share, of ownership of a corporation.

Stockbroker: a person who buys and sells stock on behalf of an investor.

Stock certificate: a document that shows ownership of a specified number of shares of stock in a corporation. Today, many companies no longer issue paper stock certificates.

Stock exchange: an organization that provides facilities for stocks to be bought and sold. It may be a physical place (like the New York Stock Exchange) or electronic (like Nasdaq).

Stock market: not a place, but the business of buying and selling stocks.

Stop orders: an order from a customer to buy or sell a stock when it reaches a certain point. Once the price of the stock passes that point, the order becomes a market order.

Term: the amount of time for which an investment is held. For bonds, the term is the time from the day the bond is issued until the day the money must be returned to the lenders.

Thinly traded stock: a stock that has very few investors.

Ticker symbol: an abbreviation unique to each stock. Ticker symbols help brokers know they are talking about the correct stock.

Trading floor: the open space where the trading of listed stocks and bonds takes place at the stock exchange.

Trading posts: the places on the trading floor where the actual buying and selling take place. Every stock is assigned to a specific trading post and is traded only at that post.

Treasury bills (T-bills): short-term US government bonds that mature in less than one year. T-bills are purchased for less than their face value. An investor receives interest when a bond is redeemed for its full face value at its maturity.

Treasury Inflation-Protected Securities (TIPS): US government bonds that are designed to protect an investor against inflation.

Treasury notes and treasury bonds: US government bonds that are sold at their face value. Investors receive interest payments every six months until the bonds mature. Treasury notes mature in two to ten years. Treasury bonds mature in thirty years.

Two-way auction: buyers make bids for what they want to pay and sellers make offers for what they want to receive until a price agreeable to both is reached.

Volatility: the unpredictability of the value of an investment over time.

Wall Street: in financial terms, the entire business of investing; also a street in New York City.

OTHER SOURCES FOR FINANCIAL VOCABULARY

Economics section on about.com

http://economics.about.com/cs/econometrics/l/blglossary.htm

Investopedia

www.investopedia.com/categories/stocks.asp?viewed=1

Museum of American Finance

www.moaf.org/resources/educational_materials/CurriculumGuideFinancialMarkets/_
res/id=sa_File1/Curriculum%20-%20Financial%20Markets.pdf

New York Stock Exchange

www.nyse.com/glossary/Glossary.html

INDEX